The Civil War Lover's Guide to New York City

Bill Morgan

SB

Savas Beatie
California

Library of Congress Cataloging-in-Publication Data

Morgan, Bill, 1949-
The Civil War lover's guide to New York City / Bill Morgan. — First edition.
pages cm
Includes bibliographical references and index.
ISBN 978-1-61121-122-1
1. New York (N.Y.)—History—Civil War, 1861-1865. 2. New York (N.Y.)—Guidebooks. 3.
Historic sites—New York (State)—New York—Guidebooks. I. Title.
F128.18.M673 2013
973.709747'1—dc23
2013008800

SB

Published by
Savas Beatie LLC
989 Governor Drive, Suite 102
El Dorado Hills, CA 95762
Phone: 916-941-6896

(E-mail) customerservice@savasbeatie.com

05 04 03 02 01 5 4 3 2 1
First edition, first printing

Unless otherwise noted, photos were either taken by author or from his collection.

Savas Beatie titles are available at special discounts for bulk purchases in the United States by corporations, institutions, and other organizations. For more details, please contact Special Sales, P. O. Box 4527, El Dorado Hills, CA 95762, or you may e-mail us at sales@savasbeatie.com, or visit our website at www.savasbeatie.com for additional information.

For Judy
viaggiatore emirto

THE
Civil War
Lover's
GUIDE TO
New York City

Contents

Contents *(continued)*

Introduction

On February 25, 1860, a little-known Illinois politician by the name of Abraham Lincoln arrived in New York City to deliver a speech to the Young Men's Central Republican Union in the new auditorium at Cooper Union. No one recognized him as he walked along Broadway to his hotel near City Hall, where he was to revise much of his "right makes might" speech. Lincoln himself would later say that it was that speech that made him president. Five years later, Lincoln's body lay in state under the rotunda of that very same City Hall, and more than a half million people waited to file past the catafalque of their assassinated leader. On April 25, 1865, the entire city was draped in black for the funeral procession of the man who died at the hands of John Wilkes Booth, brother of New York's most prominent Shakespearean actor, Edwin Booth. "A Nation Mourns" read the banner over the steps of City Hall as millions poured into the city to line the streets to bid Lincoln farewell.

In many ways, these two events frame the Civil War era, and it is surprising that very little literature focuses on the role that New York City played in that war. Of course, no great battle took place in the city, but much of the tumultuous history of the period played out here. As the largest city in the nation, New York sent more troops to the war than any other—and lost more men as a result: nearly 100,000 soldiers from the city marched off; more than 10,000 never returned. As America's publishing center, New York's newspaper and magazine editors played a crucial role in shaping public opinion, both for and against Lincoln and the war. As the capital of commerce, New York produced the materials of war, manufacturing everything from uniforms to ironclads like the USS *Monitor*. Wall Street banks financed the war, making millions in the process. And after the war, New York became a prime location for memorials and monuments to the victors. By 1865, the city had recovered from the financial setbacks caused by the loss of the cotton trade and was prospering because of the war. Business interests began to rival those of London and Paris in importance, and New York left other American cities behind in the provincial dust. As Kenneth T. Jackson, professor of history at Columbia University, has said about the city's urban growth during that period, "The result would probably have been the same even if President Lincoln had somehow avoided war, but there can be little doubt that the foundation for New York's industrial, financial, cultural, and commercial supremacy had been strengthened by the conflict between 1861 and 1865. And over those four years New York City and State made it possible for the United States to remain one nation."

When I began work on this book, I considered using a controversial title such as "New York: The Largest City of the Confederacy" to express the Southern sympathies shared, at least initially, by many New Yorkers. But that would only obscure the real purpose of the guide, which is to lead people to Civil War sites around the five boroughs. Still, it is surprising to learn that a large majority of the voters in New York City were not supporters of "Mr. Lincoln's War." In fact, the fiercest civilian rebellion to ever take place in America was the New York Draft Riots of 1863. At the outset of war in 1861, many people felt that the conflict would destroy business and the economic backlash would ruin the city's prosperity. New York was tied to the Southern economy more than any other city in the North. Southern businessmen owed tens of millions to Northern banks, and on behalf of the latter institutions some feared that if war came and the South refused to honor those debts, the losses would create a financial panic on Wall Street. When Lincoln was elected, New York's mayor, Fernando Wood, proposed that the city secede from the United States and become a free city, placing it in a position to continue doing business with both North and South. On Lincoln's inauguration day, Wood refused to fly the American flag over City Hall. It was not until Lincoln's death that the slain president became a martyr popular with the majority of people of the city.

What surprised me most when I began collecting notes for this book 25 years ago was that no one had ever set down a guide to all of the places of Civil War interest in New York City. I believe that the city has more monuments, markers, forts, homes, public memorials, buildings, graves, museum exhibits, and relics of the Civil War era than any other place in the country. It is interesting to note that Generals Grant, Sherman, Scott, McClellan, Hancock, Sickles, and others all lived in the city at one time. Even more surprising, I learned that General Robert E. Lee, Stonewall Jackson, and Mrs. Jefferson Davis lived here for extended periods. The famous Confederate song "Dixie" was first performed in a New York theater, the ironclad was invented and built here, *The Red Badge of Courage* was written here, and Grant's tomb is here. The country's most beautiful Civil War monuments, by artists such as Augustus Saint-Gaudens, Daniel Chester French, J. Q. A. Ward, and Gutzon Borglum, stand in the city's parks, and countless Civil War-era homes, businesses, forts, and public buildings still survive in a city that is constantly changing.

A study of the demographics of New York City prove that the city center has constantly been on the move northward. When the original Dutch settlers arrived on Mannahatta, they established a trading village at the very southern tip of the island. In the early years of the settlement, the residents of Nieuw Amsterdam built a wall at the northern edge of the town, which eventually became Wall Street. As the population grew, the city expanded beyond the wall, and farms and country houses began to dot the countryside below what is today 14th Street. Still, up to the Revolution Greenwich Village was no more than pastoral acreage. But late in the eighteenth century people fleeing from yellow fever and cholera epidemics in the city proper began to build homes there, and the northward expansion began in earnest. In 1807, a visionary map that would be adopted as the Commissioners' Plan of 1811 was drawn up. It projected a grid plan for all future streets north of Houston. Few people believed that there would actually be a need for streets numbering well into the hundreds; but, just in case, the town fathers made a survey and allowed for cross streets from 1st Street up to 220th Street.

By 1860, the eve of the Civil War, the population of New York (and the Bronx) had grown to 814,000, making it the largest city in the nation. Brooklyn was the third-largest city with 267,000 residents; it would not become part of New York City until 1898, when Queens and Staten Island also consolidated to form the five boroughs of the current city. For comparison's sake, New Orleans was the only Southern city in the top ten, and it had a population of just 169,000. New York's population was beginning to fill in the new blocks above 14th Street, with the wealthiest people building their homes along Fifth Avenue and spreading east and west from there. Real estate speculators were busy trying to make areas around Gramercy Park and Madison Square desirable by building new townhouses and providing mass transportation to the work centers in Lower Manhattan. For the most part, retail businesses were located along Broadway and heavier industries took up the areas along the riverfronts. During the Civil War, there were only a few scattered buildings in the blocks north of 42nd Street; so sparse was the population there that the city allowed the production and storage of explosives in factories built north of 62nd Street during the war. After the war, the creation of large works such as Central Park, Grand Central Station, and St. Patrick's Cathedral gave impetus to continued northward expansion, so monuments erected at the end of the nineteenth century in honor of Civil War veterans are often found north of 57th Street. As Manhattan became more and more residential, heavy industries found it easier to conduct business in the boroughs and eventually closed their operations along the waterfronts.

This guide is divided into geographical segments listing sites from south to north in each of eight areas. The boroughs are covered separately and the islands surrounding the city have a section of their own, even though technically they are part of one borough or another. The maps and accompanying text provide locations, but visiting hours always seem to be in flux and should be verified before making a long trip to see a particular site. There is no charge for access unless otherwise stated. Due to the large area covered by the city, allow ample time to reach each destination, and grouping locations into smaller walking tours would be appropriate only within Manhattan; for transportation to sites in the outer boroughs, I suggest public transportation or automobiles. An appendix contains short discussions of a few significant events that are linked to multiple sites covered in the book; in the text, these sites are marked with an asterisk.

This book grew out of my own interest in the Civil War and slowly developed over the years. As I took friends on walking tours of the city, I realized that many people pass by Grand Army Plaza, Lincoln Center, and Sheridan Square every day without thinking about the history behind those places. It wasn't until I was sitting in the grand lecture hall at Cooper Union—unchanged since the day Lincoln spoke from that same stage in 1860—that I decided to put it all together in one guide. Finding the sites and locations 150 years later became a challenge and an adventure, one that has taken me to all parts of the city, from Gracie Mansion on the Upper East Side to the free black community of Weeksville in Brooklyn. I hope this book will help others enjoy visiting unusual parts of the city and enthuse in the history of the Civil War that still resonates on her streets.

Bill Morgan
Bennington, VT

Acknowledgments

This guide could never have been completed without the enthusiastic support and cooperation of an army of people. I wish to thank those troops for their help and support at every turn. In the case of this book, libraries from coast to coast played a significant role in the collection of information and I wish to thank all librarians in general for their assistance. The New York Public Library and the Williams College Library were especially helpful and a great deal of my research was carried out in those two institutions. The author also wishes to thank Bill Keogan of St. John's University Library, who acted as my private librarian and was always willing to help me uncover obscure bits of information about one Civil War location or another.

Many people patiently helped sift out important facts that turn up in the following pages. Special thanks is due to Gordon and Kathy Ball, Richard Connor, Charles Dewey, William Gargan, Robert Guarino, Jack Hagstrom, Peter Hale, Joe Hall, Tim Moran, Alan Petrulis, Stephen Sandy, and Pat Young for their insightful suggestions. Whenever a question of fact arose, I turned to historical societies, museums, and libraries for help, visiting internet sites only as a last resort. I owe a large debt of gratitude to those people and institutions: Justin Batt at the Harbor Defense Museum; Elizabeth Call at the Brooklyn Historical Society; Sarah Clark at the Staten Island Historical Society; the people at the Flushing Cemetery Association; Kathy Haines at the Center for American Music; Danielle Hilkin at the Queens Historical Society; Harold Holzer at the Metropolitan Museum of Art; Kathleen A. McAuley at the Bronx County Historical Society; Jason Radmacher at the John Street United Methodist Church; Marcus Romero at the Brooklyn Museum; Lois Rosebrooks at the Plymouth Church; Andrew St. John at the Church of the Transfiguration; David C. Sibley at St. John's Episcopal Church; Raymond Wemmlinger at The Players; and Timothy Wroten at the New-York Historical Society.

Gratitude is also extended to my publisher, Savas Beatie. Theodore P. Savas had the foresight to see the value of this guide and helped in the production. Mr. Beatie also had the wisdom to select Rob Ayer to act as my editor, a job he has done with great knowledge and care. Lindy Gervin, Veronica Kane, and Sarah Keeney have all worked tirelessly editing, designing, and promoting this work. Their improvements would delight any author and I would like to thank them all.

And as always, I would like to acknowledge Judy Matz, my lifelong collaborator, without whom, this and all my labors would be meaningless. For decades she has worked as my sounding board and first editor, shaping my poor prose into understandable sentences and correcting embarrassing mistakes before anyone knew they had been made. To her this work is dedicated.

Manhattan

I. Downtown: South of Worth Street

001. JOHN ERICSSON MONUMENT
Battery Park, northeast of Castle Clinton near Battery Place

In 1903, a second version of a statue depicting the inventor John Ericsson (1803–1889) was unveiled in Battery Park. The first version had been dedicated in 1893, but the sculptor, Jonathan Scott Hartley (1845–1912), had been unhappy with that effort and revised his work at his own expense. The larger-than-life bronze statue of Ericsson stands on a granite pedestal on which four relief tablets are mounted. In Ericsson's left hand is a model of his most famous creation, the USS *Monitor*, and in his right he holds the design blueprints. The bronze reliefs on the base depict Ericsson's most important inventions, which include the screw-propelled warship, the rotary gun carriage, and a steam-driven fire engine.

Ericsson was a Swedish-born inventor who arrived in New York in 1839 and lived in the city for 50 years. From 1844 until 1864, he lived in a building that once stood at 95 Franklin Street near Church Street. On March 9, 1922, a tablet was affixed to that house identifying it as the site where the inventor designed the first ironclad, the USS *Monitor*. The building has since been demolished and the plaque has disappeared. At the same time, another plaque was placed on the building in which he lived from 1864 until his death in 1889. That location, 36 Beach Street, has now been renamed Ericsson Place in his honor. The plaque there was also destroyed when that building was demolished and replaced by a newer loft building. It included these lines from a letter Ericsson wrote to Abraham Lincoln volunteering to help preserve the Union: "I seek no private advantage or emolument of any kind. Attachment to the Union alone impels

Statue of John Ericsson.

me to offer my services at this fearful crisis, my life if need be in the great cause which Providence has called us to defend."

As a naval engineer, Ericsson answered the Union's call to design a new type of fighting vessel. During the first days of the Civil War, news had reached the North that the Confederates were refitting the old USS *Merrimack* with an iron shell that would withstand artillery fire. The Southerners rechristened the resulting vessel the CSS *Virginia*, although it would be forever remembered in history as the *Merrimack*. Initially the Union's Navy Board was skeptical about the seaworthiness of Ericsson's monitor design, but the inventor was confident and commissioned three different companies to manufacture parts for the ship. The *Monitor* was quickly assembled during the winter of 1861-62 and arrived at the mouth of Chesapeake Bay just in time to defend the Union naval blockade of Richmond and Norfolk from attack by the *Virginia*.

The fight between the two ironclad warships, the USS *Monitor* and CSS *Virginia*, was perhaps the most important naval conflict of the entire Civil War. On March 9, 1862, they engaged in battle near the towns of Hampton and Newport News, just north of Norfolk. For nearly four hours they fired at each other at point-blank range. In the end, the two ships fought to a draw, which meant the South could not break the blockade. Later the *Monitor* sank in a storm off Cape Hatteras and the *Virginia* was scuttled by her crew to avoid capture by Northern troops. Realizing the importance of the ironclad, the Union Navy hastily built 66 more, making wooden-hulled warships obsolete.

002. PIER 13, NORTH RIVER
Albany and West Streets, looking west

(Top) Rescue of a Fugitive Slave; (Inset) Reward Poster.

The Hudson River, or North River as it is known to sailors, extended inland as far east as West Street during the Civil War. In the past 150 years, all the area west of that street has been reclaimed from the river, but piers once lined the west side of the street. Pier 13 met West Street at the foot of Liberty near present-day Cedar Street and extended for a few hundred yards into the river. There are records of several smuggling incidents that took place on that particular pier.

One involved a runaway slave who had been captured under the Fugitive Slave Act of 1850 and was being returned to his owner, a Mr. Jameson of Lynchburg, Virginia. Two deputy marshals attracted a large antislavery crowd at Pier 13 when they attempted to drag the man to the SS *Yorktown*, then ready to weigh anchor. A policeman intervened and asked to see their papers, which the marshals had left in their carriage. While one of the marshals went for the papers, the slave managed to escape from the other and ran off up West Street, much to the delight of the crowd.

During the war, Pier 13 was also frequently used by gun smugglers. On one occasion, five cases of muskets were found waiting to be loaded onto the SS *Mexico*, a steamer bound for Havana. Customs officials stopped the shipment because they knew that the weapons would be transferred in Cuba to a blockade runner that would take the guns to a Southern port, after which they would be used to kill Union boys. This was not an isolated incident: many shipments of contraband weapons succeeded in making their way through the port of New York to Southern destinations.

003. JAMES HAMLET'S WORKPLACE
58 Water Street, mid-block between Cuyler's Alley and Old Slip

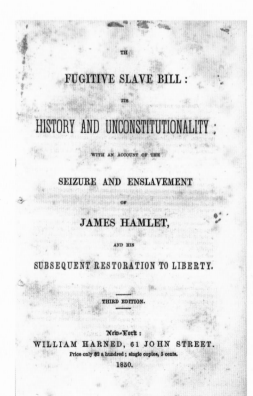

In September 1850, the first black man to be seized under the infamous Fugitive Slave Act of 1850 was James Hamlet, who lived in the Williamsburgh section of Brooklyn. At the time, he was a porter with the firm of Tilton and Maloney, then at 58 Water Street, and it was here that he was arrested. Mary Brown of Baltimore had sent Thomas J. Clare to New York to track down an escaped slave, and Clare said that Hamlet was his man, although it was later proven that Hamlet had been born a free black man. Under the law (which was supported, by such otherwise enlightened Northerners as Daniel Webster, as part of a compromise with southern states), Hamlet was not allowed to testify in his own defense. On October 1, 1850, a large crowd supportive of Hamlet attended a meeting at Mother Zion Church, the oldest black church in the city, where the audience took up a collection to buy his freedom.

John H. Woodgate, a white businessman, went to Baltimore and ransomed Hamlet for $800,

Title page of Hamlet's book.

$100 of which had been contributed by another free black man, Isaac Hollenbeck. As a result of the Hamlet case, free blacks in the city formed a vigilante group they called the Committee of Thirteen. Their goals were to prevent future kidnappings and to assist fugitive slaves. The case attracted a great deal of publicity and helped bring the humanitarian issues associated with the Fugitive Slave Act to the public's attention.

004. J. & W. SELIGMAN AND COMPANY BUILDING
1 William Street, at the intersection with South William Street

Joseph Seligman.

In 1846, Joseph Seligman (1819–1880) and his brothers founded J. & W. Seligman and Company. By 1859, the family had established an import house and opened a dry goods store in New York, with headquarters in a building that once stood at 1 William Street, now replaced by newer offices. At one point as many as 2,500 people were employed to manufacture garments. During the Civil War, Seligman manufactured and sold uniforms to the Union army and also became involved with the sale of bonds. His financial connections in Germany enabled him to sell $200 million in bonds on behalf of the U.S. government. After the war, his family firm got out of dry goods and focused all its attention on banking. The historian W. E. Dodd wrote that Seligman's sale of bonds in Europe was "scarcely less important than the battle of Gettysburg." As a result, Seligman became one of the wealthiest "robber barons" of the latter half of the century.

005. SOUTH STREET SEAPORT MUSEUM
Fulton and South Streets. Hours and general information: www.seany.org or (212) 748-8725. Admission charge.

The South Street Seaport Museum is a great place to learn about the maritime history of New York City and how it related to the Civil War. Many exhibits and displays feature objects from that era, and its collection of sailing ships, although not exactly from the period, give you an idea of the nature of seaport activity at the time. It is interesting to note that by the 1860s New York shipping firms were beginning to lose business to European steamships. Although New York shipbuilders remained loyal to the faster American clipper ships that had been built to rush prospectors to the California gold fields at the end of the 1840s, more dependable steamships were beginning to make them obsolete. War also meant that ships sailing under the American flag were susceptible to attack by Confederate raiders, so European companies began to take over much of the international business. American shipping never recovered from those setbacks, and although the port itself remained very busy it was merchant vessels flying foreign flags that filled the harbor, much as they do today.

The Heartland Brewery on the corner at 2 Fulton Street was known as Sweet's for more than 150 years. That restaurant was thought to have been established in 1845 as A. M. Sweet & Son, Hotel and Restaurant. Sweet's was a popular hangout for "blackbirders," the name given to slave smugglers. Even though slavery had been outlawed in New York in 1827, it did not stop the slave traffickers. They often met here to discuss how they would unload their secret human cargoes and transfer them to railroad cars for the long trip south.

(Top) Sailing ships on display at
the South Street Seaport Museum;
(Left) Site of Sweet's Hotel
and Restaurant.

006. TRINITY CHURCH

Broadway at Wall Street. Hours: M–F 7:00 a.m. – 6:00 p.m., Sat 8:00 a.m. – 4:00 p.m., Sun 7:00 a.m. – 4:00 p.m. General information: www.trinitywall street.org or (212) 602-0800.

Like all churches, during the Civil War period Trinity Church played an important role in the spiritual lives of its parishioners. As one of the city's oldest and most distinguished churches, Trinity was the focal point of many wartime observances, and its bells chimed for Northern victories. Ship riggers raised an American flag on top of the 281-foot spire (the tallest structure in the city until 1890) so that it could be seen from all points in the city. In 1861, the congregation turned out to cheer volunteer units marching down Broadway on their way to defend Washington during the first few days of the war. When the 6th Massachusetts Regiment band struck up the song "Yankee Doodle," the crowds hoorayed wildly from the church steps. The rector of Trinity from 1862 until 1908 was Dr. Morgan Dix (1827–1908), and All Saints' Chapel on the northwest corner was added in his honor in 1913; it contains a beautiful memorial to the church's wartime pastor. Just inside the sanctuary to the right of the main entrance is a memorial to U.S. Navy officer Captain Percival Drayton (1812–1865). The plaque documents his service in the battles of Port Royal, Mobile Bay, and the 1863 siege of Sumter. At the latter he commanded the ironclad *Passaic*, which is depicted on the marker. Drayton's brother, Thomas F. Drayton, was a classmate of Jefferson Davis and became a general in the Confederate army. Ironically, he was the commander of the forts destroyed by his brother at Port Royal in November 1861.

Outside in the churchyard are the graves of several Civil War soldiers. On the north side near the Broadway fence is a memorial in honor of six firemen of Empire Steam Engine Company No. 42 who were killed in battle during the war. On the south side of the church is a monument to Capt. James Lawrence (1781–1813), whose dying command given during a battle in the War of 1812, "Don't give up the ship!" is well known. Lawrence's wife, Julia Montaudevert Lawrence (1788–1865), is buried beside him and is mentioned on the west side of his

(Inset) Morgan Dix;
(Above) Postcard view of Trinity Church, ca. 1899.

monument. She lived through the Civil War period and sewed American flags for the Northern cause. Once when someone disparaged her efforts, she chased him out of the house with a lint knife. Onlookers forced the offender to kneel and cheer the flag as penance. Lieutenant Thomas J. Jackson (1824–1863), later known as Gen. Stonewall Jackson, visited New York on his honeymoon in the summer of 1857. Like many tourists, he and his wife, Mary Anna Morrison Jackson, climbed to the top of Trinity's tall steeple to enjoy the bird's-eye view of the city.

007. U.S. SUB-TREASURY BUILDING (FEDERAL HALL NATIONAL MEMORIAL)
26 Wall Street, at the corner of Nassau Street. Hours: M–F 9:00 a.m. – 5:00 p.m. General information: www.nps.gov/feha or (212) 825-6990.

The building that originally stood on this spot served as the first capitol building of the United States, hence the statue of George Washington being sworn in as president. By 1862, it had been rebuilt and served as the U.S. Customs House. That year the Customs House moved from this imposing 1842 classical revival building to new quarters at 55 Wall Street. The U.S. Sub-Treasury then took over the white marble building until 1920, at which point the building became a museum.

(Top right) John Cisco; (Above) Federal Hall.

During the Draft Riots in 1863, the Sub-Treasury was filled with millions of dollars in Union gold and silver, making it a certain target for looters. In response to the threat, John Cisco, the assistant treasurer, armed his employees with guns, hand grenades, and bottles of vitriol to throw from the windows if attacked. At the height of the disturbances, the building was protected by a group of untrained recruits from the Brooklyn Navy Yard, but the mob never made it as far as Wall Street to test their mettle. The original vaults in which the Union stored gold can still be seen. On display is the police command log of the 18th Precinct, the station house at 127 Wooster Street that was burned to the ground during the Draft Riots on July 14, 1863. The log book was the only object saved from the flames.

008. JOHN STREET UNITED METHODIST CHURCH
44 John Street. Hours and general information: www.johnstreetchurch.org or (212) 269-0014.

The John Street United Methodist Church, established in 1766, houses the oldest Methodist congregation in America. The current building, built in 1841, is the third to be erected on the same site, re-using roof timbers and foundation stones from the previous buildings. Among the members of the early congregation was a slave named Peter Williams, Sr. (1749–1823). He served as church sexton, doing maintenance work around the church, keeping the grounds, and digging graves. Following the Revolution, when his Tory owner returned to England, the church trustees purchased Williams and allowed him to work off the money spent for his freedom. In 1796, rebelling against segregation within the church itself, Williams helped a group of black worshippers establish the African Methodist Episcopal Zion Church. They officially chartered the new church in 1810 as the first black church in New York. Williams went on to become a successful tobacconist, and his son, Peter Williams, Jr. (1780–1840), became the first African-American Episcopal priest in the city.

John Street United Methodist Church.

009. ASTOR HOUSE
Broadway between Vesey and Barclay Streets

The most luxurious hotel in New York City during the Civil War was the Astor House, once located near City Hall on the west side of Broadway between Barclay and Vesey Streets. It had more than 300 rooms and occupied the entire block. It has since been replaced by an even larger structure named the "Astor Building." In its day, the five-story Astor House sported Greek Revival columns that opened onto an opulent lobby off of which were gardens and dining rooms,

President-elect Lincoln's arrival at the Astor House, 1861.

all exquisitely decorated. It was the preferred hotel for Abraham Lincoln (1809–1865) and his wife, Mary Todd Lincoln (1818–1882), whenever they visited the city. Lincoln's first visit to the hotel was in July 1857, when he and Mary visited New York City as tourists. He returned again in February 1860, and in his hotel room put the finishing touches to his Cooper Union speech, the speech that would propel him onto the national political stage and lead to his nomination for president. On his way to Washington a year later as president-elect, Lincoln was officially escorted from the train station down Broadway to the Astor House. He sat in an open coach pulled by six black horses and was greeted by a cheering crowd, even though the city had voted overwhelmingly against him. Mary enjoyed staying in the elegant hotel on her shopping trips to the city throughout the war years, usually without her husband. She visited the city a dozen times during his four years in office.

On the night of November 25, 1864, Confederate conspirators set fire to 13 hotels in the city, including the Astor House, hoping to burn down the city, but the staff quickly brought the fire under control with only minor damage.

010. BARNUM'S AMERICAN MUSEUM
222 Broadway, at the corner of Ann Street

A visit to view the curiosities at Barnum's American Museum on the southeast corner of Broadway and Ann Street was one of the most popular pastimes in the city during the Civil War. From 1842 to 1865, the sensationalized attractions mounted by impresario P. T. Barnum (1810–1891) were on display here for anyone who could pay the 25-cent admission. An estimated 38 million people did just that, more than the population of the whole country at the time. Even Mary Todd Lincoln visited the museum on her husband's 1861 trip to the city as president-elect. Barnum was the quintessential showman: he filled his museum not only with geological displays, collections of birds and animals, scientific inventions, curiosities, and historical dioramas, but also with the sort of freaks and varied acts that today would be associated with a circus sideshow. Among his most popular attractions were Chang and Eng, the Siamese twins; General Tom Thumb, the 25-inch-tall dwarf; and Miss Jane Campbell, the giant girl. Miss "Major" Pauline Cushman appeared in the museum's lecture hall for a few weeks and held the audience spellbound

Barnum's American Museum.

with her tales about spying for the Union army in Nashville. Barnum even displayed a wax figure of Jefferson Davis dressed in petticoats and another of Robert Cobb Kennedy, the Confederate who tried to burn down the city. The lecture hall at the museum was one of the city's largest, and it regularly provided performances of theatrical productions such as *Uncle Tom's Cabin*.

When Confederate saboteurs tried to set fire to the city's hotels in 1864, they also threw an incendiary bomb into the stairway of Barnum's Museum, but it failed to do much damage, and Barnum boasted that his museum was fireproof. But that obviously wasn't the case, because the museum burnt to the ground the following year, on July 13, 1865, in a spectacular blaze. Yet even the devastating fire had its humorous side: when one employee tried to salvage the figure of Jefferson Davis from the flames, it was snatched from his arms and carried off to be hung in effigy from a lamp post in front of St. Paul's Church across the street.

011. CITY HALL PARK
Broadway at Park Row

During the Civil War, the park just south of City Hall was used as a recruiting station, a barracks, and an army hospital. The barracks were 400 feet long and as many as 2,000 recruits at a time stayed in them temporarily, but they were built hastily of rough wood. Similarly, each company formed in the city had its own recruiting center, but it was often nothing more than a large tent or shack. New troops were continually being drilled on the lawn in front of City Hall

City Hall Park recruiting office, 1864.

before leaving for battle. Shortly after Lincoln's call for troops, more than 6,000 Irish immigrants volunteered for service with the 69th New York Regiment. The raw recruits were dispatched immediately to protect the capital in Washington from attack, marching down Broadway to waiting ships. Crowds lined the sidewalks and cheered enthusiastically. Walt Whitman watched from the steps of the Astor House and later wrote about the soldiers going off to war as young men and "returning with thinn'd ranks, young, yet very old, worn, marching, noticing nothing."

012. CITY HALL
Broadway near Murray Street. General information: (212) 639-9675.

In 1803, the foundation stone for City Hall was laid on the site of New York's old almshouse, and the building has been the seat of city government ever since. During the Civil War, City Hall bore witness to a great deal of drama. In April 1861, Elmer Ellsworth (1837–1861) organized a regiment from the ranks of New York City volunteer firemen. Before the major battles of the war ever took place, Ellsworth became the first commissioned officer to die when he was shot taking down a Confederate flag that was flying over an Alexandria, Virginia, hotel. His death shocked many in New York, who hadn't expected the war to amount to much. His body was carried back to the city and laid in state in the Governor's Room at City Hall. It was the same room in which just a few months earlier President-elect Lincoln had met with Mayor Fernando Wood (1812–1881) and members of the Common Council to assure them that he would never consent to "the destruction of this Union."

Unfortunately, City Hall would be used for Lincoln's own wake four years later, perhaps the most solemn observance to be held in the building. Following his assassination, Lincoln's body traveled by train and ferry to New York City, arriving on April 24, 1865. At the Desbrosses Street dock his body was transferred to a glass-sided hearse drawn by six gray horses. The procession, led

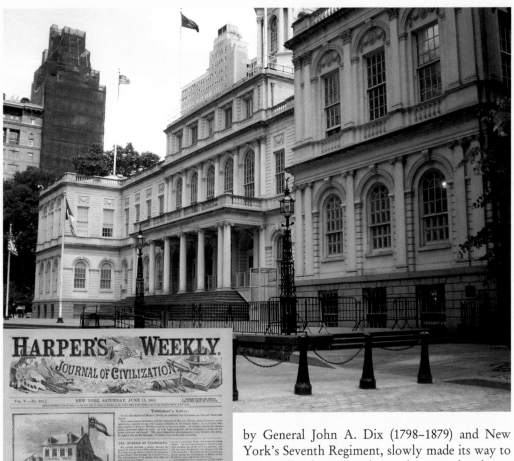

(Top) City Hall; (Above) The Death
of Colonel Elmer Ellsworth.

by General John A. Dix (1798–1879) and New York's Seventh Regiment, slowly made its way to City Hall, where Lincoln's casket was placed on a catafalque. The city virtually shut down and an endless line of people streamed past the bier to pay their last respects to the fallen president. Not everyone in the city was in mourning, however: there were reports of groups of Irish immigrants who cheered the news of his death. The next day a funeral car pulled by sixteen horses took Lincoln's body to the Hudson Railroad Depot to continue the journey to Springfield, Illinois, for burial. As proof that emancipation was not complete, the City's Common Council originally forbade black people to participate in the procession, but at the last minute reached a compromise that gave a small contingent of freedmen permission to bring up the rear. On August 5, 1885, thousands of mourners viewed the body of Ulysses S. Grant at City Hall, and several years later the body of General Abner Doubleday was also laid out here, in a simple oak coffin draped with the flag he took down from Fort Moultrie in 1861.

Today not only Lincoln's portrait but those of other Civil War notables, including Mayors Wood, Opdyke, and Gunther, and even Lincoln's opponent General George B. McClellan (1826–1885), are part of the city's collection of artworks that decorate City Hall.

013. HORACE GREELEY STATUE
City Hall Park, northeast of City Hall near Centre Street

Just to the east of the Tweed Courthouse is the larger-than-life bronze statue of a seated Horace Greeley (1811–1872) by noted artist John Quincy Adams Ward (1830–1910). The pedestal was designed by the architect Richard Morris Hunt (1827–1895) and dedicated in 1890. The likeness is nearly perfect—it was modeled after a death mask of Greeley. The famous editor founded the *New York Tribune*; the statue portrays him holding a copy on his knee. Originally the work was placed in front of the *Tribune* Building on the northeast corner of Nassau and Spruce Streets across from City Hall Park, but it obstructed traffic heading toward the Brooklyn Bridge,

Statue of Horace Greeley.

so was moved to this location in 1916. The *Tribune* Building had been designed by Richard Morris Hunt as well, but was demolished in 1966.

Greeley moved to New York ten years before he began publishing the *Tribune* in 1841, and during the 1850s he lived in a house no longer standing at 35 East 19th Street. By the time the Civil War began, he was one of the country's best-known newspaper editors. With 300,000 readers, the paper had the largest circulation of any in the world, and under Greeley's leadership it helped shape national political opinion. The editorial position of the newspaper was strictly Republican, in favor of both Lincoln and abolition at the start of the war. It was Greeley's opinion that if the South wanted to secede the North should let it, an unusual position for a Northern newspaper. It might have been said that Greeley did not favor Lincoln as much as he disliked Lincoln's opponent, William H. Seward (1801–1872). "Anyone but Seward," became Greeley's motto during the early campaign. Since the *Tribune* supported Lincoln, the newspaper agreed to print the entire text of his 1860 Cooper Union speech. In order to make certain that it was done correctly, Lincoln visited the newspaper to see Amos Jay Cummings, the proofreader for the *Tribune*, and went over the galleys on the day that he delivered his important speech. Mr. Cummings later regretted that after the final version was approved Lincoln's handwritten manuscript was thrown into the trash.

Greeley was also famous for his support of the Homestead Act, about which he is often quoted as having said, "Go west, young man!" (although in truth he never said it). As an old man in 1872, he retired from the newspaper to run for president against U. S. Grant. He was defeated by an overwhelming margin, and the disappointment of the loss contributed to his death a few weeks after the election. Another statue in honor of Greeley was erected near Macy's and is described later in this book.

014. A. T. STEWART'S DRY GOODS EMPORIUM
280 Broadway and Chambers Street

A. T. Stewart's Dry Goods Emporium.

In 1846, Alexander T. Stewart (1803–1876) opened America's first great department store in this Italian renaissance palace devoted to shopping. The building still stands on the northeast corner of Broadway and Chambers Street. During the Civil War era, it was popular with the ladies because of the wide variety of merchandise to be found under one roof—not to mention Stewart's staff of handsome male clerks, called "Stewart's nice young men." When Mary Todd Lincoln, a notorious shopaholic, was given $20,000 by Congress to renovate the White House, she went on a shopping spree at Stewart's, Haughwout's, and a few other businesses along Broadway. During the four years of her husband's presidency, Mrs. Lincoln made many shopping trips to New York, piling up a mountain of debt.

015. AFRICAN BURIAL GROUND NATIONAL MONUMENT
Duane Street between Broadway and Elk Street. Hours: M–Sat, 9:00 a.m. – 4:00 p.m. General information: www.africanburialground.gov or (212) 637-2019.

In 1991, while construction workers waited to begin digging the foundation for a new office building at the corner of Duane and Elk Streets, archaeologists began to uncover skeletons in what is now known to have been the African Burial Ground. It took an act of Congress to halt construction and turn a small portion of the lot into a permanent memorial to those buried here. A visitor center and small museum are located in the new building that faces Broadway. From

African Burial Grounds.

1712 to 1794, New Yorkers of African descent were buried on six acres of ground set aside solely for the "Negro Burial Ground." An estimated 10 to 20 thousand people were buried here, many of whom had been brought to America as slaves. In the earliest days of the city, slaves were buried in a potter's field located near the present Trinity Church. Laws passed in the early eighteenth century made burial more difficult for black people. The regulations stated that no more than twelve people could be present at the burial of a black person, and interments had to take place in daylight. These requirements were contrary to some African tribal customs. By the time of the Civil War, the cemetery had been forgotten, and various buildings, including a fire station, had been erected on the site.

016. PRINTING HOUSE SQUARE AND NEWSPAPER ROW
Park Row east of City Hall Park

At one time, New York City had more than twenty daily newspapers, and during the Civil War years the area just to the east of City Hall Park was the headquarters for most of them: the *Times*, *Tribune*, *Herald*, *World*, and *Sun* newspapers all clustered around Park Row. Today the statue of Benjamin Franklin (1706–1790) (who was a printer and publisher of newspapers himself) is one of the few relics left to commemorate this area as the media center of its day. The construction of the Brooklyn Bridge in 1883 and urban renewal wiped out many vestiges of the once-thriving newspaper row, but a few sites remain. Pace University now uses the old *New York Times* building at Park Row and Spruce Street for classes, but it is an 1889 construction that replaced the Civil War-era *Times* building that stood on the same site.

Printing House Square, 1868.

When the Confederates opened fire on Fort Sumter in April 1861, New Yorkers were caught off guard and wanted the news as quickly as possible. Crowds congregated in this area and eagerly read each new edition as it was nailed to public signposts in Printing House Square. The police had to be called out to keep the streets open so that the newspapers could be delivered to the rest of the city. A few weeks earlier, crowds had gathered to wait for the election returns. They learned that Lincoln had lost the city by 30,000 votes but still managed to carry the state despite the shortfall. Lincoln did not fare much better in the 1864 election: he lost the city vote again, this time to Gen. George McClellan.

When the Draft Riots erupted in the summer of 1863, the mob threatened to attack those newspapers that favored Lincoln and the Union. The owner of the *New York Times*, Republican Henry Raymond (1820–1869), a staunch Lincoln supporter, joined his employees in a makeshift army to protect the building. They manned three Gatling guns (an early form of machine gun) and prepared to do battle from the windows and roof. Horace Greeley at the *New York Tribune*, whose offices were on the northeast corner of Spruce and Nassau Streets, would not allow his workers to carry weapons because he did not want to cause harm to fellow citizens. His gesture did not keep the mob from attacking, and they ransacked the building, nearly burning it

Statue of Benjamin Franklin.

down in the process; the police intervened just in the nick of time. The *Tribune* employees armed themselves against the rest of the disturbances and further attacks. Surprisingly, by the time of the riots Greeley had already turned against Lincoln and was searching the ranks of politicians for someone to replace him.

Many of the newspapers in the city from the outset were sympathetic to the South and feared that a war would be bad for business and hence bad for the city. The editor of the *New York Daily News*, then at 19-21 Chatham Street, was Mayor Fernando Wood's brother Benjamin, a staunch anti-Republican. He believed that electing Lincoln and "forcing" the South to secede was the biggest mistake the country had ever made. Another paper, the *New York World*, was later shut down by the Union Army for disloyalty when it published pamphlets critical of Lincoln and his policies. Editor James McMaster of the *Freeman's Journal* went so far as to aid the Confederate conspirators who came to firebomb the city in 1864. After their first visit to his offices at 5 Tryon Row, one block east of City Hall Park, the editor continued to secretly meet with the conspirators at his home.

During the Civil War, the *New York Sun* was located on the southwest corner of Nassau and Fulton Streets. It was perhaps the most conservative newspaper in the city, and during the early years of the war it was edited by members of a religious group that held prayer meetings in the city room at noon each day.

017. BURDICK BROTHERS, PUBLISHERS
8 Spruce Street

Hinton Rowan Helper.

Hinton Rowan Helper (1829–1909) was a Southern critic of slavery who, according to one of his contemporaries, became the "best known and worst hated man in America." In 1857, he finished the manuscript of the book *The Impending Crisis of the South: How To Meet It*. In the book he pointed out that slavery hurt the economic prospects of the majority of Southern people. Unable to find a publisher for his book in the South, he contacted the firm of Burdick Brothers in New York at 8 Spruce Street, which was willing to take on the controversial book. However, Burdick Brothers made Helper personally guarantee to pay the expenses of printing if the book failed to sell. The book became an instant success, selling more than a hundred thousand copies in the first year alone. Over time the book went through several editions and became the number one bestseller for Burdick. Later the Republican party issued an abridged version and distributed several million copies as a campaign giveaway.

Fellow Southerners believed that Helper's ideas fostered a division between people within the South to the benefit of the North, so he was ostracized at home. Even those who merely read his book were criticized, and an angry mob hanged three men in Arkansas for owning copies. Surprisingly, Helper was a racist who hated slaves and did not want to see them set free—he wanted them returned to Africa. His belief was simply that slavery hurt white Southerners more than it helped their economy. When Lincoln took office, he appointed Helper consul to Argentina for the duration of the war. After several business reversals, Helper committed suicide in 1909.

018. CURRIER & IVES
152 Nassau Street, at the corner with Spruce Street

THE ASSASSINATION OF PRESIDENT LINCOLN.
AT FORD'S THEATRE WASHINGTON, D.C. APRIL 14TH 1865.

The Assassination of President Lincoln, by Currier & Ives.

The most famous of the many lithographers at work in New York during the Civil War period were Currier & Ives, who had a shop at 152 Nassau Street and printed their wonderful artworks on the third, fourth, and fifth floors of the building that once stood on the corner of Nassau and Spruce. The partnership of Nathaniel Currier (1813–1888) and James Merritt Ives (1824–1895) began in 1857 and continued for the rest of their lives. From their offices here they produced hundreds of quality prints that became extremely popular in mid-nineteenth century America. Today they are collectors' items and sell for thousands of dollars each, but originally most sold for less than a dollar apiece. Currier & Ives advertised themselves as "Publishers of Cheap and Popular Prints," focusing on average families who could afford to decorate their walls with their prints. Many of the pictures depicting Civil War scenes were grossly inaccurate, but the public found their racist images of black American life amusing. The prints do give us a glimpse into everyday life during the war. Currier & Ives became the most popular and prolific lithographers during the Civil War, and their prints of Lincoln during his life and subsequent to his assassination sold widely.

019. LYDIA MARIA CHILD AND THE *ANTI-SLAVERY STANDARD*
142 Nassau Street

Lydia Maria Child.

Although writer, editor, and journalist Lydia Maria Child (1802–1880) is not well known today, she was one of the most famous women of her era. In the early 1830s, she became a follower of William Lloyd Garrison (1805–1879) and supported his abolitionist politics. One of her first books was called *An Appeal in Favor of that Class of Americans Called Africans*. From 1841 to 1843, as the editor of the *National Anti-Slavery Standard* she influenced public opinion in favor of abolition. During this period, she lived in New York at the Park Hotel at 142 Nassau Street, now gone. She stayed on in New York at other addresses and published columns that were collected in her book *Letters from New York* in 1845. Child was a champion of liberty and freedom, and throughout her life she worked to bring justice to oppressed peoples.

In 1859, after John Brown's raid on Harpers Ferry, Lydia Child published her letters in support of Brown's cause in the *New York Tribune*.

020. HARPER & BROTHERS
327-335 Pearl Street

Not many buildings are left from the middle of the nineteenth century, when the area around Franklin Square was the publishing center of New York. The offices of Harper and Brothers, then at 327 Pearl Street, are no exception. The firm was founded in 1825 by brothers James, John, Fletcher, and Wesley, and by the time of the Civil War it had become one of the country's foremost publishers of books and magazines. *Harper's Magazine* and *Harper's Weekly* circulated to hundreds of thousands of people during the war, and illustrations by artists such as Winslow Homer, Thomas Nast, and Livingston Hopkins became very popular with their readership. Harper's tried to take a middle-of-the-road position on the issue of slavery, and as a result was often referred to as "Harper's Weakly." During the presidential election of 1860, the editors supported Stephen A. Douglas against Abraham Lincoln, but when war broke out they wholeheartedly backed the Northern cause. After the war, *Harper's Weekly* supported Republican candidates such as Ulysses S. Grant in his bid for the presidency.

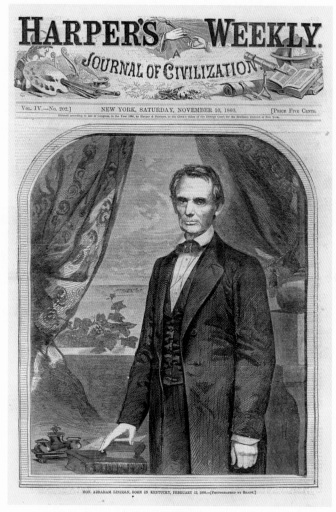

Harper's Weekly.

021. BROOKS BROTHERS CLOTHING STORE
Corner of Catherine and Cherry Streets

Established in 1818 in a building that once stood on the northwest corner of the intersection of Cherry and Catherine Streets, Brooks Brothers was one of many businesses that helped make this area the center of the clothing industry. The firm earned a reputation for providing high-quality clothing for men and pioneered the concept of making clothes in standard sizes instead of tailoring each item for the customer. It is surprising therefore to learn that during the Civil War, Brooks Brothers produced substandard uniforms for the troops. In 1861, the New York State Military Board gave the company a contract to produce 12,000 uniforms at $19.50 each. When the manufacturers could not find enough affordable cloth to fill the contract, they proposed to use a new material made from recycled scraps mixed with glue, called "shoddy."

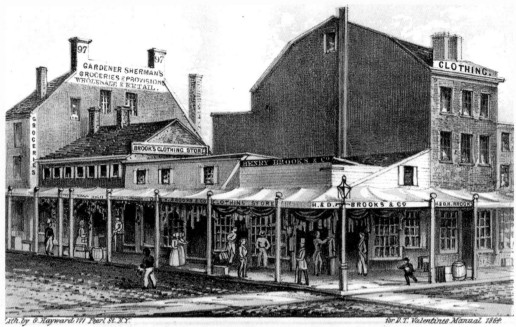

BROOKS CLOTHING STORE, CATHARINE ST. N.Y. 1845

Brooks Clothing Store on Catharine Street.

Unfortunately, although shoddy looked good on the shelves, it was not sturdy and fell apart in bad weather; it was not the sort of material to be used on the field of battle. To their credit, Brooks Brothers replaced the inferior uniforms with ones of better quality at their own expense, but after newspapers reported the incident the word "shoddy" became synonymous with inferior quality merchandise.

Throughout the war, many prominent men purchased their clothing at Brooks Brothers. Among their clientele were Generals Grant, Hooker, Sheridan, and Sherman. Abraham Lincoln also frequented the store and wore a Brooks Brothers topcoat to his second inauguration in 1864. Sadly, it was also the coat he was wearing the night of his assassination at Ford's Theater the following year.

During the second day of the Draft Riots in July 1863, the rioters began to loot stores and businesses throughout the city. As a prominent merchant, Brooks Brothers became a prime target, and the mob attacked their original store at Catherine and Cherry Streets. The police drove them off once, but the looters returned as soon as the police moved elsewhere. They ransacked the store and looted $50,000 in merchandise before the police were able to clear the shop. One officer was shot in the face during the melee. Brooks Brothers closed their location here in 1874 and the site became part of a public park, but the firm continues in business to this day.

II. Downtown: Between Worth and Houston Streets

022. NEW ENGLAND HOTEL
30-38 Bowery

The New England Hotel was yet another of the hotels that the Confederates set ablaze on the night of November 25, 1864, in their unsuccessful attempt to burn down the city. The actual location of the hotel is difficult to determine; maps from the era identify only small, separate buildings here. The New England Hotel, at different times called the American Hotel and the Home Hotel, stood north of the corner of Bowery and Bayard, and probably extended into the adjacent buildings, which was common at the time. The old buildings still standing at numbers 40 and 42 Bowery

(Top) 40 Bowery today;
(Left) Stephen Collins Foster.

might even have been part of the hotel; although that seems unlikely, they do give some idea of what the building might have looked like.

More significantly, the New England Hotel is the place where songwriter Stephen Collins Foster (1826-1864) was living when he fell and fatally gashed his head. Foster was one of the most popular composers of the nineteenth century, and his songs were loved in both North and South. He wrote classic songs such as "Camptown Races," "Swanee River," "My Old Kentucky Home," and "Beautiful Dreamer" during a time when songwriters had no way to protect the distribution of their output because music copyrights went largely ignored. As a result, others often pirated Foster's work and he reaped few financial gains for his songs—his estimated payment for "Oh! Susanna" was less than $100.

Although Foster was born and raised in western Pennsylvania and it was there that he wrote his most famous songs, many people mistakenly believe he was from the South. In fact, Foster was only south of the Mason-Dixon Line twice in his life, once on a honeymoon trip to New Orleans. Many of his songs were performed right here on the Bowery in blackface minstrel shows, a highly popular form of entertainment at the time. In 1860, Foster moved his family to New York City, still trying to earn a living as a songwriter. Initially he settled at 6 Greenwich Street (that building, like the New England Hotel, is long gone), but a year later his wife and daughter left him to return to Pittsburgh. Foster turned to drink and moved into the less expensive New England Hotel on the Bowery for 25 cents a night. While living here in January 1864, Foster collapsed and suffered a severe injury in the fall. He died three days later on January 13 in New York's Bellevue Hospital at age 37. He had 38 cents in his pocket.

023. MATHEW BRADY STUDIO
359 Broadway, between Franklin and Leonard Streets

Mathew Brady (1822-1896) is the best known photographer of the Civil War. In 1841, he was apprenticed to Samuel F. B. Morse (1791-1872), the inventor of the telegraph, who was also accomplished in the use of the daguerreotype, an early version of the photograph. Brady opened his own studio on Broadway near Fulton in 1845, but by 1854 moved to 359 Broadway, near Franklin. On the top three floors of the building still standing there, he installed a lab, a portrait studio, and a gallery of photographs of famous people. On February 27, 1860, the day of Abraham Lincoln's Cooper Union speech, the future president bought a new silk top hat and came to Brady's studio to sit for a portrait. The photo was used for all his publicity during the campaign. Lincoln is quoted as having said, "Brady and the Cooper Union speech made me president." The following month, Brady moved uptown to 643 Broadway, and it was there that many Civil War generals came to pose for portraits, including Grant, Buell, Burnside, Farragut, Hooker, McDowell, McClellan, Meade, and Sherman. Brady also photographed leading Confederates, including Jefferson Davis, P. G. T. Beauregard, Stonewall Jackson, and Robert E. Lee. Lincoln returned to Brady's studio several times, sitting for the famous portraits that are now used on the $5 bill and the penny.

During the war, Mathew Brady and his assistants visited many of the battlefields and took pictures that

Mathew Brady's studio today.

document the wide scale of the war in both its humanity and inhumanity. Brady himself came so close to the action at the first battle of Bull Run that he was nearly captured. After the war, Brady hoped that the government would buy his collection of 10,000 photographic plates recording the conflict, but it did not, and he fell into bankruptcy. He ended up living in a cheap rooming house that still stands at 127 East 10th Street and died penniless in the charity ward of New York's Presbyterian Hospital in 1896.

President Lincoln and his son Tad, by Mathew Brady.

024. DAVID RUGGLES HOME AND BOOKSTORE
36 Lispenard Street, on the corner of Church Street

David Ruggles (1810-1849) was a free-born black abolitionist from Connecticut who moved to New York City in 1826 at the age of 16. He became involved with the Underground Railroad, and in 1835 helped found the New York Committee of Vigilance, whose mission was to help free slaves. The group did this in part by providing information to slaves who were held in New York. By law, any slave kept in New York for more than nine months was entitled to his freedom, but slaves had to know this in order to exercise their rights. This type of activity created many enemies for Ruggles, some of whom attempted to kidnap him and sell him into slavery in the South.

Ruggles originally worked as a sailor and grocer. By 1838, he had settled down to live at 36 Lispenard Street in a building which still stands on the southeast corner of Lispenard and Church Streets. A marker was recently placed on the

David Ruggles.

UNDERGROUND RAILROAD STATION
36 LISPENARD STREET

ON SEPTEMBER 3, 1838, HUMAN-RIGHTS ACTIVIST FREDERICK DOUGLASS
ESCAPED SLAVERY IN MARYLAND BY DISGUISING HIMSELF AS A SAILOR
AND TRAVELING NORTH BY CARRIAGE, TRAIN, AND BOAT. A FEW DAYS
LATER HE ARRIVED AT 36 LISPENARD STREET, THEN A SMALL BRICK
BUILDING AND A "STATION" OF THE UNDERGROUND RAILROAD, A
NETWORK OF SECRET "CONDUCTORS" AND SAFE-HOUSES FOR FUGITIVE
SLAVES. HERE, AFRICAN-AMERICAN ABOLITIONIST DAVID RUGGLES
KEPT A READING ROOM AND OPERATED A PRINTING PRESS WHERE HE
PUBLISHED ANTI-SLAVERY MATERIAL, INCLUDING *MIRROR OF LIBERTY*,
AN ABOLITIONIST NEWSPAPER. THE SITE ALSO SERVED AS
HEADQUARTERS OF THE NEW YORK VIGILANCE COMMITTEE, ONE OF
THE NATION'S MOST ACTIVE ANTI-SLAVERY CAMPAIGNS, WHICH AIDED
MORE THAN 1,000 FREEDOM-SEEKING MEN, WOMEN, AND CHILDREN.

NEW YORK LANDMARKS PRESERVATION FOUNDATION
2006

Historical marker on 36 Lispenard Street,
once the shop of David Ruggles.

building to commemorate his residence. By that time, he was running his own African-American bookstore and library just down the street at 67 Lispenard in a building no longer standing.

Ruggles is credited with helping over 600 slaves escape to freedom during his short lifetime. The list included the most famous black abolitionist of them all, Frederick Douglass (1818–1895). A few days after gaining his freedom, Douglass married Anna Murray, a free black woman, in a small ceremony held in Ruggles' shop. Out of the same shop Ruggles edited the country's first black magazine, *The Mirror of Liberty*, from 1838 to 1841. Poor health forced Ruggles to retire to Massachusetts, where he died at the age of 39.

025. NEW YORK STATE SOLDIER'S DEPOT CONVALESCENT HOME AND HOSPITAL
50-52 Howard Street

Remarkably, at 50-52 Howard Street stands the actual building that housed returning wounded soldiers during the Civil War. The state of New York set aside $200,000 for the relief of furloughed and discharged soldiers, a figure supplemented by the federal government and private donations. At this site the wounded had available to them a hospital, dispensary, and surgery in addition to bathing rooms, a barber shop, kitchen and dining rooms, a dormitory, and quarters for nurses. New York was a tough town even then, and one of the goals of the hospital was to help protect veterans from robbery and theft while they were recovering. The depot remained active until it closed in April 1866, having served nearly 150,000 soldiers over the course of the war.

Early in the war, the poet Walt Whitman (1819-1892) volunteered to nurse sick soldiers back to health here. In

50-52 Howard Street.

1862, when his brother was injured in battle, he went to Washington to find him at a similar hospital. Whitman was a loyal Unionist, and many of his poems deal directly with the war and wounded soldiers. While living in Washington, Whitman often saw President Lincoln in the streets and came to admire him greatly. After Lincoln's assassination, Whitman wrote some of his best work about the fallen leader, including the poem "O Captain! My Captain!"

026. D. DEVLIN AND CO. STORE
459-461 Broadway, at the corner of Grand Street

During the Civil War, shopping was no longer limited to walk-in trade. Many larger companies began to make fortunes through mail order, selling via catalogues to all parts of the country. D. Devlin and Co. built its temple of commerce at 459 Broadway in 1860-1861. Originally they manufactured and sold clothing, so during the war it was easy for them to expand their business to include uniforms, employing over 2,000 workers in the process. Volunteers from as far away as Minnesota equipped their men entirely with purchases from Devlin. Daniel Devlin, the proprietor, provided the uniforms for New York's famous Irish Brigade out of his own pocket. Devlin's became well known for selling everything from socks to cartridge belts at a reasonable price. Although merchants had been worried that the war would hurt business, within a few years it was apparent there were fortunes to be made. Then as now, war was good for business.

459-461 Broadway today.

027. BROOKES' HALL
361 Broome Street, between Elizabeth and Mott Streets

In January 1861, meetings protesting Lincoln's election and the Republican party in general took place at Brooke's Hall. The *New York Times* identified the organizers as being mostly Irish and members of the "Working Men's Anti-Republican In-Aid-Of-South-Carolina-Party." Shouts such as "Kill Lincoln" and "Hang the Republicans" rang out during meetings here. The speakers

An Anti-Republican Demonstration in New York City, 1860 [near 625 Broadway].

proclaimed that the city would lose $20 million a month of Southern business if war erupted; their real fear was that freed black men would take jobs away from immigrants. (In fact, the opposite became the rule, as employers favored white Irishmen over former slaves.) At the end of the meetings, six cheers were given for South Carolina and three groans for Horace Greeley, whom they hated even more than Lincoln. Recently a new building has been erected on this site.

028. MECHANICS' HALL
472 Broadway

Mechanics' Hall was built in 1803 as the headquarters of the Mechanics' Society. Originally they held their monthly meetings here, but by the 1840s it had been converted into a theater seating as many as 2,500 people. For decades the theater featured blackface minstrel troupes, which were the rage in prewar New York. Although we now find these shows to be racist and offensive, they were the popular venues that brought many memorable songs to the attention of the American public. Stephen Collins Foster's songs were a mainstay of Christy's Minstrels, who bought the building in 1847. Foster's songs included "My Old Kentucky Home," "Old Black Joe," and "Old Folks at

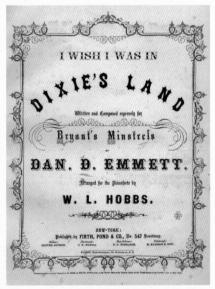

Dixie's Land sheet music.

Home," all of which became favorites in the South. In 1857, the Bryant Minstrels played in the hall for the first time. A few years later, Dan Emmett, a white composer, introduced his new song "Dixie" to their audiences. Recently scholars have pointed out that Emmett probably learned the song from two black musicians named Ben and Lew Snowden. On February 26, 1860, Abraham Lincoln attended Bryant's minstrel show and was delighted to hear the new tune. He asked that they play "Dixie" again, and they did. In 1866, the building burnt and was replaced.

029. E. V. HAUGHWOUT AND COMPANY
488 Broadway, at the corner of Broome Street

In 1856, Eder Haughwout built his department store at 488 Broadway. The building, designed to resemble a Venetian palace and constructed of cast iron, was spectacular. The following year, Elisha Graves Otis (1811-1861) installed the first passenger elevator in America in this store to whisk customers from floor to floor. In recent years, there has been a great deal of attention focused on the shopping habits of Mary Todd Lincoln. She had an uncontrollable urge to spend

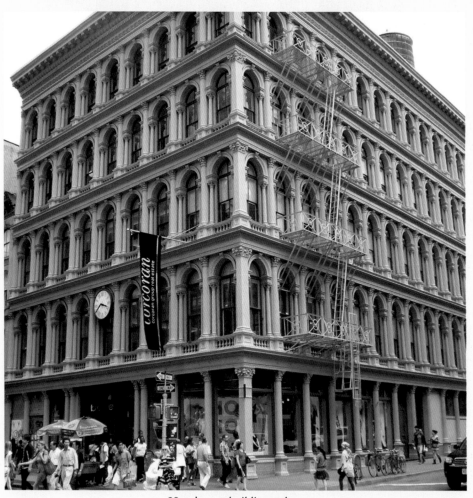

Haughwout building today.

money, and managed to spend more money than her husband made as president. But merchants gave her unlimited credit—and she took advantage of it. Congress gave Mrs. Lincoln $20,000 to spend on White House renovations, and she spent some of it at Haughwout's on two 190-piece Haviland dinner services. One set was custom-made with the great seal of the United States, the other set featured her own initials. The government paid for both.

030. U.S. SANITARY COMMISSION
498 Broadway

498 Broadway today.

At the outset of the war, it became evident that the government could not provide for the medical needs of so many soldiers. As a result, President Lincoln created the U.S. Sanitary Commission (USSC) to coordinate volunteer efforts aimed at providing food, clothing, and medical supplies to the troops. It grew out of the Women's Central Relief Association of New York and was supported by donations and fund-raisers such as the large sanitary fairs that communities mounted during the war years. The Commission's headquarters were in a building that still stands at 500 Broadway, and although the work of raising money was done mainly by women the administration was completely male. Henry W. Bellows, the pastor of All Souls Church, served as president; Frederick Law Olmstead, the designer of Central Park, was the first executive secretary; and the lawyer-diarist George Templeton Strong was the treasurer. Many scholars have suggested that the Sanitary Commission was the most important organization produced during the war years. Later the USSC maintained offices in other places, including at 823 Broadway, but that building is gone.

031. ST. NICHOLAS HOTEL
507-527 Broadway, at Spring Street

A thousand guests could lodge on Broadway at the St. Nicholas Hotel during the Civil War. A small portion of the giant building still stands at 521-523 Broadway. In 1853, it opened as a luxurious six-story hostelry catering to residents and out-of-town visitors alike. The hotel building itself was so large that its stables, laundry, and other buildings took up a large part of Mercer Street directly behind the hotel. Elaborate chandeliers and mirrors decorated every public room. Even the War Department took space in the St. Nicholas when its headquarters building at 37 Bleecker Street became too crowded. General John Wool (1784–1869) set up his command post here during the Draft Riots in 1863, and both the governor and the mayor stayed here, seeking U.S. Army protection against the mobs that roamed the city. The bar boasted its own telegraph office so that men did not have to leave to conduct their business affairs. Although the St. Nicholas was favored by Southern businessmen before the war, this was one of the 13 hotels the Confederate conspirators set on fire on November 25, 1864, and it was the only one that suffered significant damage. Still, the saboteurs fell far short of their goal of burning down the city.

Portion of St. Nicholas Hotel as it appears today.

032. CONTINENTAL MONTHLY OFFICES
532 Broadway

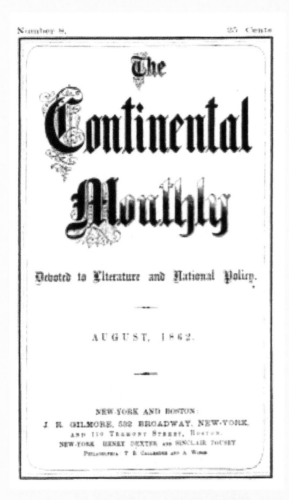

In January 1862, James R. Gilmore (1822–1893), a personal friend of Abraham Lincoln, began to publish *The Continental Monthly*, a periodical "Devoted to Literature and National Policy," at 532 Broadway in a building no longer standing. With Charles Godfrey Leland (1824–1903) as editor, the magazine was staunchly pro-Union and antislavery. Although it only lasted until 1864, it was influential in supporting the policies of the president. Leland was a popular humorist and folklorist who edited the magazine until he enlisted in the Army; shortly thereafter he fought in the battle of Gettysburg. Gilmore used the magazine to publish his own articles, many of which dealt with the issue of slavery. These were collected into two volumes, *Among the Pines* and *My Southern Friends*, both of which reached a wide audience. In 1898, Gilmore published his memoir, *Personal Recollections of Abraham Lincoln and the Civil War*, which gives an intimate, if not always accurate, picture of Lincoln.

Title page of *The Continental Monthly*.

033. TIFFANY'S JEWELRY STORE
550 Broadway

Tiffany's was founded in 1837 at 259 Broadway, but by 1853 it had expanded so much that the company built a new marble building at 550 Broadway, where it did business throughout the Civil War. The centerpiece of the new building was a clock held on the shoulders of a 9-foot tall, bronze-coated wooden statue of Atlas. It still guards the entrance to Tiffany's flagship store, now located at Fifth Avenue and 57th Street. That figure was carved by H. F. Metzler, a carver of ship figureheads. During the war, Tiffany's produced high-quality swords, military insignia, and medals for soldiers and designed flags for various regiments. In honor of Abraham Lincoln's inauguration, Tiffany's fulfilled a commission to make a silver presentation pitcher for the new president. For the same occasion, Lincoln purchased a beautiful seed-pearl jewelry suite for his wife Mary from the store. After the war, Tiffany's made many presentation swords for officers, from Admiral Farragut to Generals Grant and Sherman.

Tiffany's clock on Fifth Avenue at 57th Street today.

034. OLD ST. PATRICK'S
263 Mulberry Street, Prince Street between Mulberry and Mott Streets. Hours and general information: www.oldcathedral.org or (212) 226-8075.

The cornerstone of the Gothic revival basilica of St. Patrick's Old Cathedral was laid in 1809, destined to anchor the city's first cathedral church. This would be the spiritual seat of the Roman Catholic church in New York until the new St. Patrick's opened in 1879 on Fifth Avenue at 50th

Old St. Patrick's.

Street. During the Civil War, the Old Cathedral was the heart of the Irish community, and as such it was the site of many celebrations and funerals. On April 23, 1861, the 69th regiment, composed mostly of Irish immigrants, was blessed here by Archbishop John Hughes before the men marched off to defend Washington, DC. It is said that the 69th was the only Union regiment not to flee from the field during the first battle of Bull Run—and suffered heavy casualties as a result. After their initial 90-day enlistment period expired, many of the men re-enlisted in the famous Irish Brigade. Their leader, Col. Michael Corcoran, was captured during the first battle, but he was later released and returned to New York. He formed additional regiments and rose to the rank of brigadier general before his death in 1863. In Corcoran's absence, Thomas Francis Meagher took over command of the Irish Brigade and recruited additional troops of Irishmen. Nearly 75 percent of the members of the Irish Brigade were killed or wounded in battle, and some of the soldiers were buried in graves on either side of St. Patrick's. Three members of that regiment were awarded the Congressional Medal of Honor. In 1866, a fire destroyed the interior of the church, but the outside walls remained standing. It was rebuilt, and the current Erben organ was installed at that time.

035. METROPOLITAN HOTEL
Northeast corner of Broadway and Prince Street

The Metropolitan Hotel was one of the first-class hotels that clustered along this stretch of Broadway during the mid-nineteenth century. Its advertisements touted the 13,000 square yards of carpet and 12 miles of gas and water pipes that supplied the two-acre building with light and running water. Confederate conspirators Ashbrook and Harrington checked into the hotel in 1864 and lived in luxury—until they attempted to burn it down. Although Mrs. Lincoln stayed at the Astor House during her visits to the city, she is said to have preferred the meals served at the Metropolitan. Nothing remains of that grand hotel today.

Metropolitan Hotel, ca. 1863.

036-037. ST. AUGUSTINE'S CHAPEL and WILLETT STREET METHODIST EPISCOPAL CHURCH

St. Augustine's: 290 Henry Street, between Jackson and Montgomery Streets. Hours and general information: www.staugnyc.org or (212) 673-5300. Bialystoker Synagogue: 7-11 Willett Street, now Bialystoker Place. Hours and general information: www.bialystoker.org or (212) 475-0165.

About the only thing in this area that survived the Civil War era are two churches: St. Augustine's Episcopal Church, originally known as All Saints Church, and the Willett Street Methodist Episcopal Church, now the Bialystoker Synagogue. All Saints was built with local

fieldstone between 1827 and 1829 as a new parish of Trinity Church. Edgar Allen Poe (1809-1849) is said to have attended services here. Of particular interest are the two slave galleries in the balcony on each side of the organ. Although slavery was abolished in New York in 1827, visitors to the church from other states were welcome to bring their slaves along to worship services. Until recently iron shackles remained here, showing how slaves were restrained to keep them from running away during the services. After the Civil War, All Saints joined with another church and became St. Augustine's.

As counterpoint to St. Augustine's Chapel with its slave gallery is the Willett Street Methodist Church. It was once an active part of

(Top) St. Augustine's Chapel; (Right) Bialystoker Synagogue.

the Underground Railroad, and as such helped to smuggle slaves from the South to freedom in the North. The northwest corner of the balcony contains a secret door concealing a ladder that leads to an attic used by fugitive slaves. Built in 1826, this building, like St. Augustine's, was constructed of local fieldstone. In 1905, the building was taken over by a Jewish congregation.

038. BARUCH PLACE
Off East Houston Street, near the FDR Drive

Although many people believe that Baruch Place was named after the financier Bernard Baruch (for whom Baruch College and the Baruch Houses are named), it was really named for his father, the doctor Simon Baruch (1840-1921). What makes Dr. Baruch interesting to fans of the Civil War is that he was an assistant surgeon in Gen. Robert E. Lee's army from 1862 to 1865. Simon was born in Germany and emigrated at the age of 15 with his family. They settled in South Carolina and he completed his education at the Medical College of Virginia in 1862. During the war he was captured by Union forces twice, once after the second battle of Bull Run and once after the battle of Gettysburg. On both occasions he was released. Following the war he practiced medicine in South Carolina before moving to New York City in 1881, where he helped found Montefiore Hospital. Dr. Baruch was a proponent of hydrotherapy and was instrumental in establishing the system of public bath houses in New York City at the turn of the twentieth century.

DR. SIMON BARUCH, LONG ILL, DIES AT 80

Pioneer in Scientific Hydrotherapy in America Was Father of Financier.

SURGEON IN SOUTHERN ARMY

Originator of Free Public Baths Here Gave Valuable Services in Camps During the War.

Simon Baruch obituary.

039. EAST RIVER SHIPYARDS
East River between Pike and East 14th Streets

U.S. Iron Clad "Roanoke" at the Novelty Iron Works.

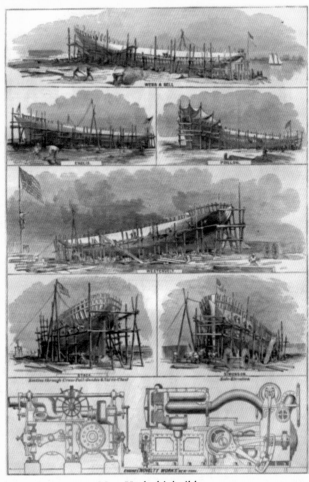

New York shipbuilders.

During the Civil War era, the area along the East River from Pike Street to 14th Street was the location of many of America's best shipbuilders. Among them were Brown and Bell, Engles, Novelty Works, Smith and Dimond, William H. Webb, and Jacob Westervelt. Several of these companies had built their reputations by making the fastest clipper ships in the world. Marine engineering changed dramatically with the invention of the ironclad warship, and the shipyards here helped make the United States the greatest naval power on earth. Following the Civil War, the shipyards moved to other locations and the waterfront was filled in, extending the land well past the present-day FDR Drive.

The Novelty Works were at 12th Street, and it was here that the USS *Roanoke* was built and launched in 1863. Twelve hundred men were kept busy at the Novelty Works refitting the ship with a thousand tons of armor and three gun turrets. The same iron works had built the turret for the *Monitor* a year earlier. The largest plant was probably William H. Webb's boatyard at 6th Street, where he built more than a hundred ships. Even during the height of the war, the company was large enough to produce ironclads for the Italian navy while still outfitting the Union fleet. During the Draft Riots of July 1863, a rumor circulated that the mob would attack Webb's shipyards to destroy the ironclad *Dunderberg*, under construction at that time. But the rumor proved to be false and the ship was launched on schedule—on July 22, 1865, too late to take part in the war. It was a 7,000-ton, 378-foot-long, ironclad frigate, the most powerful vessel of its type to date, armed with at least 18 guns. Throughout the neighborhood are tell-tale signs of the former shipyard activity, such as the name of the Dry Dock Playground and Pool at Avenue D and East 10th Street.

III. East Village

040. HOUSE OF LORDS
19 East Houston Street, at the southwest corner with Crosby Street

The House of Lords, a tavern that stood on this site along with another tavern called the House of Commons just down the street on Houston, were among the more popular bars serving the area in the last half of the 1800s. The location within a block of police headquarters was a major reason for their popularity. During the winter of 1864–65, John Wilkes Booth (1838–1865), who had long been sympathetic to the Southern cause, was approached by the Confederate secret service. They concocted a plan according to which Booth would kidnap Abraham Lincoln and the members of his cabinet and turn them over to Jefferson Davis in Richmond. As farfetched as the idea sounds, Wilkes began making plans that winter. He met with another young actor, Samuel Knapp Chester (1836–1921), at the House of Lords to discuss the plot. Afraid that they might be overhead, the two left the tavern and walked along 4th Street. Chester is said to have refused to become involved. He later testified that

John Wilkes Booth.

Booth offered him $3,000 to turn off the lights at Ford's Theater and prop the back door open on the night of the assassination. At the time of his meeting with Booth, Chester lived at or near 45 Grove Street.

041. POLICE DEPARTMENT HEADQUARTERS
300 Mulberry Street, between Bleecker and Houston Streets

In 1862, the New York Police Department moved its headquarters to a building that once stood at 300 Mulberry Street near the corner of Houston Street. In the first year of service, the building became the command center for the police as they tried to quell the disturbances of the Draft Riots of July 13–16, 1863. John A. Kennedy (1803–1873) was the superintendent of police at the time. In one skirmish on East 46th Street between Lexington and Third Avenues, he was nearly beaten to death by the mob. He was rescued by John Eagan, a respected citizen who convinced the rioters that Kennedy was already dead, then hid his "lifeless" body in his wagon. Eagan carried Kennedy to the police station, where doctors were able to save the superintendent's life. Later, 10,000 rioters marched on the building, but after a battle the police turned back the mob. Thousands were arrested and booked at this station to await trial. Woefully outnumbered, the police called in the army to restore peace to the city.

Metropolitan Police Headquarters, 1863.

042. LAURA KEENE'S THEATRE and THE WINTER GARDEN THEATRE
Keene: 622-624 Broadway; Winter Garden: 672-674 Broadway, on the corner with Bond Street.

Laura Keene (1826–1873) was a British-born stage actress who had been an early supporter of Edwin Booth (1833–1893), the brother of John Wilkes Booth, and was linked to Edwin romantically. Later she was to become Edwin's competitor. For a while, Keene was the most popular actress in America, and as an entrepreneur founded her own theater. She built and managed Laura Keene's Theatre at 622 Broadway, which rivaled Booth's Winter Garden in popularity. One of Keene's most famous roles was the female lead in "Our American Cousin," a part she played in Washington at Ford's Theater on the night of Lincoln's assassination. Surprisingly, her career suffered as a result of the incident while Booth's did not.

(Top right) Laura Keene;
(Above) Hamlet Medal awarded
to Edwin Booth.

The Players

The Winter Garden Theatre once stood on the northeast corner of Broadway and Bond Street. Before and during the Civil War, it was the home stage for Edwin Booth, America's greatest Shakespearean actor. At one point, Edwin played in *Hamlet* for one hundred consecutive nights here, a record-setting accomplishment. The Winter Garden was also the stage on which the three Booth brothers (Edwin, John Wilkes, and Junius) appeared together for the only time in a benefit performance of *Julius Caesar* on November 25, 1864. By that time Edwin had purchased the theater. Both theaters have been razed and newer structures built on the sites.

043. DEPARTMENT OF THE EAST, U.S. ARMY OFFICE
37 Bleecker Street

The administrative duties of the army were split into geographical sections, one for the Department of the East, one for the Department of the Pacific, and so on. The East, which included New England, New York, and New Jersey, was headquartered in the old brick building

that still stands at 37 Bleecker Street. All the business of the army passed through these offices, which were under the direction of Maj. Gen. John Adams Dix (1798–1879). At the outset of the war, Dix was serving as the secretary of the treasury. He won notoriety when he sent a message to the officers of the U.S. Revenue Cutter Service ship in New Orleans: "If anyone attempts to haul down the American flag, shoot him on the spot." Although he overstepped his authority with that command, it made Dix an early hero, and as a reward he was appointed commander of all volunteers on May 16, 1861. It was Dix who arrested many members of the Maryland legislature, thereby preventing that state from voting on secession from the Union. Too old to command troops in the field, he directed the Department of the East from the headquarters here from July 1863 through the end of the war. In fact, it was Dix who was put in charge of suppressing the New York Draft Riots in the summer of 1863.

For the duration of the war, all Southerners were required to register here on Bleecker while in New York; if they failed to do so, they were subject to arrest as spies. During the Draft Riots, this building was also a focal point for the mob's wrath, but the well-armed staff withstood attempts to set fire to the building.

37 Bleecker Street today.

044. PFAFF'S BEER CELLAR
647 Broadway, near Bleecker Street

Walt Whitman (1819–1892), the writer most identified with nineteenth-century New York, is also the most difficult to connect to an existing site. Nearly every building associated with Walt Whitman's 40 years in New York City is now gone. This is not surprising, since Whitman usually lived and worked in less-than-elegant surroundings, so his homes were among the first to be torn down for new development. Newspapers for which he worked prospered and moved to larger and more modern quarters, or they failed and their quarters were replaced by other buildings. But it is a mystery why no statues or plaques commemorate his life in the city, since his poetry extols the vitality of the city more than the work of any other writer of his time.

However, the Manhattan building that housed his favorite saloon, Pfaff's, managed to survive. Several writers have reported various addresses for Pfaff's, some of which have been torn down, but the New York Historical Society confirmed that 647 Broadway was the true location of the cellar where Pfaff's operated. That building is still here, though greatly changed. Now a new bar called "The Vault at Pfaff's" is at 643 Broadway. It was in Pfaff's Beer Cellar that author and editor William Dean Howells (1837–1920) first met Whitman in 1860, although Howells was a teetotaler and did not drink. An early biographer wrote of their meeting: "Whitman, white-haired and bearded, looking closer to eighty than forty, wearing an open-necked shirt and a homespun suit, is leaning back in his chair and casually shaking hands with a young, slim, formally dressed Howells, who is bending

647 Broadway today.

slightly toward the poet, as though paying court. Howells later came to understand Whitman, the rough poet of New York's streets, in terms of his own Boston-adopted gentility: 'The apostle of the rough, the uncouth, was the gentlest person; his barbaric yawp, translated into the terms of social encounter, was an address of singular quiet, delivered in a voice of winning and endearing friendliness.'"

Walt Whitman.

During the years when Whitman frequented Pfaff's tavern, he was the editor of the *Brooklyn Eagle*, but he resigned in 1847 over a dispute with the publisher: unable to convince his employer to support the antislavery ticket in the upcoming election, Whitman threw the publisher down some steps. Whitman was passionate about everything he did, and his support for the Union's cause was no different. In September 1861, Whitman read his *Beat! Beat! Drums!* aloud in Pfaff's. During the Civil War, he left the city to help nurse the wounded in a Washington military hospital, and he was devastated when he heard of Lincoln's death. During Whitman's later years, he became known as the "good grey poet." He moved to Camden, New Jersey, and continued to write until his death in 1892.

045. DR. JOEL SHEW
47 Bond Street

One popular form of treatment for a wide variety of illnesses and pain during the nineteenth century was "the water cure," or hydrotherapy. It was so common that the professional magazine *Water-Cure Journal* had 50,000 subscribers by 1852. The method of cleansing the body through drinking and bathing in mineral water was practiced in New York by many people, including Dr. Joel Shew (1816–1855) and his wife Marie Louise. Doctor Shew published a book on the subject, a comprehensive work with an especially long title: "The Water-Cure Manual: Descriptions of the various modes of bathing, the hygienic and curative effects of air, exercise, clothing, occupation, diet, water-drinking, etc." He and Marie established a treatment facility in their home at 47 Bond Street in 1843. Interestingly, one of their patients was Thomas "Stonewall" Jackson, who sought relief from his ailments before the war began. The building still stands and now houses a restaurant.

47 Bond Street today.

046. MERCHANT'S HOUSE MUSEUM
29 East 4th Street. Hours: Th–M, noon – 5:00 p.m. www.merchantshouse.com or (212) 777-1089. Admission charge.

The interesting thing about the Merchant's House Museum is that the original contents of the house have not been disturbed in a hundred years. The house was built in 1832 by Joseph Brewster, who sold the house to Seabury Tredwell in 1836 for $18,000. It became a museum in 1936 after Tredwell's daughter Gertrude passed away. The Tredwells were the only family to live in the house for nearly a century. Tredwell was a merchant and a relative of the Vanderbilts, but not directly involved in the war. The family preserved the nineteenth-century building intact, both inside and out, and Gertrude spent her last years there as a recluse. After her death, the house was purchased and preserved as a museum. Stepping across the threshold, a visitor can walk back in time to experience a house just as it was in the mid-nineteenth century.

Merchant's House Museum.

047. SAMUEL SULLIVAN COX STATUE
Tompkins Square Park, near the corner of East 7th Street and Avenue A

The 1891 statue of Congressman Samuel Sullivan Cox (1824–1889) in Tompkins Square Park was donated by postal workers because Cox worked on their behalf to raise their salaries. The bronze standing figure was sculpted by Louise Lawson (186?–1899), one of America's first female sculptors. It stands on a granite pedestal that identifies Cox as the "postman's friend." Cox is interesting as a Civil War footnote as well. In 1864, he was one of Gen. George McClellan's most faithful supporters in his unsuccessful bid for the presidency against Abraham Lincoln. Cox strongly believed that McClellan's election was essential to bringing about a quick resolution to the war. His efforts helped McClellan win the city vote in a landslide, but the general lost the statewide and national races to Lincoln.

Statue of Samuel Sullivan Cox.

048. ISAAC T. HOPPER HOME
110 Second Avenue, between East 6th and East 7th Streets

This beautiful Greek Revival townhouse was built in 1839 for one of the most famous antislavery activists in America, Isaac T. Hopper (1771–1852). Hopper was a successful Quaker businessman who helped at least a thousand black people escape slavery via the Underground

Isaac T. Hopper house.

Railroad during his lifetime. At one point, a slave catcher seized Richard Allen (1760–1835), the black minister who founded the African Methodist Episcopal Church, and threatened to take him back to the South in chains, even though Allen was not the fugitive slave he was looking for. Hopper helped to successfully defend Allen, then counseled Allen to sue the slave catcher for false arrest. Isaac and his daughter Abigail Hopper Gibbons (1801–1893) devoted their lives to helping others, and after her father's death Abigail converted their home into a halfway house for women recently discharged from prison. Living in New York, Isaac Hopper opened an abolitionist bookstore on Pearl Street and also formed the New York Association for Friends, an agency to assist the victims of slavery. Since many ex-slaves were illiterate, Hopper was instrumental in helping them write stories about their lives, including the narrative, *Twelve Years a Slave*, written by Solomon Northrup, a free black man who had been kidnapped by slave traders.

049. McSORLEY'S OLD ALE HOUSE
15 East 7th Street. General information: (212) 474-9148.

McSorley's Old Ale House.

According to the sign in the window, McSorley's bar first opened in 1854 and has never closed. John McSorley came from Ireland's County Tyrone and served in the Union army as a member of the 69th Regiment. The owners of McSorley's are proud that the bar is almost unchanged since the days of the Civil War, and it is well worth a visit for that reason alone. The potbellied stove, sawdust on the floor, and wanted poster of John Wilkes Booth will convince you that you have stepped back into the nineteenth century. Although scholars dispute it, many believe that Abraham Lincoln stopped at McSorley's after he gave his famous speech at the nearby Cooper Union.

050. SEVENTH REGIMENT ARMORY
East Side of Third Avenue between East 6th and East 7th Streets

The New York Militia's Seventh Regiment was nicknamed the "Silk Stocking Regiment" because so many of its members were from the city's wealthy high society. In 1860, the regiment moved into a new three-story, cast-iron building that it shared with the Tompkins Market across from the Cooper Union: the regiment used the upper floors of the building for military drills and office space while the ground floor housed butchers and produce merchants. When war was declared, the "Darling Seventh" was one of the first regiments called up for a 30-day tour of duty, and left the armory on April 19, 1861, heading for Washington. The members numbered 1,050 and many more thousands came to cheer them off. "On no other occasion has the excitement been so intense, so sublime and almost terrific. New York was certainly raving mad with excitement," wrote one participant. One newspaper reported that it was the best-appointed regiment in the country, dressed in gray uniforms with white cross belts. Led by wealthy businessman Col. Marshall Lefferts (1821–1876), the regiment saw limited action and lost only one man, a Private Keese, who was actually killed by the accidental discharge of a musket. His body was returned to New York to be buried in Green-Wood Cemetery. Several times during the war the Seventh Regiment was pressed into active service for short periods, usually doing guard work and rarely

Seventh Regiment marching off to war, 1861.

assigned to the front. In 1863, it was called upon to defend the city from the mob during the Draft Riots. An ultra-modern building now stands on the site of the armory.

051. COOPER UNION
Cooper Square, Third Avenue between East 7th and East 8th Streets. General information: www.cooper.edu or (212) 353-4100

The Cooper Union was founded in 1859 to provide free higher education to students based solely on merit. The school's founder, inventor Peter Cooper (1791–1883), used his considerable wealth to set up the institute. A beautifully executed monument to him by Augustus Saint-Gaudens (1848–1097) can be found near the East 7th Street entrance. On February 27, 1860, Abraham Lincoln appeared at the Cooper Union to deliver a speech in the Great Hall in the basement of the main building. The hall held 1,500 people and was selected because it was one of the largest auditoriums in the city at the time. It remains today much as it was in 1860 when Lincoln spoke there. More than anything else, Lincoln's speech led to his nomination for the presidency. "Let us have faith that right makes might," Lincoln said that evening. The newspaper editor Horace Greeley said the speech was the most convincing argument to restrict the extension of slavery he had ever heard. Because of the press coverage, the little-known Lincoln awoke the next morning to find himself a famous man and the front runner for the Republican nomination.

Cooper Union.

Other notable people of the period spoke in the Great Hall, including Henry Ward Beecher, Frederick Douglass, William Lloyd Garrison, Ulysses S. Grant, the abolitionist Wendell Phillips, Harriet Beecher Stowe, and Mark Twain. Not all rallies held at the Cooper Union were as liberal. Fernando and Benjamin Wood used the podium to speak to what they called Peace Democrats, but whom the *New York Times* referred to as "the Anti-Negro-Submission Party." "This is a government of white men and established exclusively for the white race," said then-Congressman Fernando Wood.

Cooper Union historical marker.

The Women's Central Association of Relief was organized at the Cooper Union. Out of this group sprang the U.S. Sanitary Commission that provided medical help, supplies, clothing, and food for the troops during the Civil War. The Ladies Committee met every day and opened a storefront on the Third Avenue side of the building to help support these efforts financially.

052. BIBLE HOUSE
Fourth Avenue between East 8th and East 9th Streets

Bible House.

The block-square Bible House, built in 1858 by the American Bible Society on Fourth Avenue at Astor Place, became one of the largest book publishing centers in New York, employing nearly 600 people. The society distributed 85,000 Bibles to the troops during the first year of the war alone. In addition to Bibles, it published hymnals, spiritual tracts, and a host of other books. In 1864, a year before the Civil War ended, publishers asked Horace Greeley to write a multivolume history of the war. Greeley agreed and was given office space and a secretary at the Bible House for that purpose. Every morning he worked on his book for a few hours before going on to his newspaper office for a full day of editorial business. That same year the first volume was published as *The American Conflict: A History of the Great Rebellion in the United States of America*, followed by the second volume in 1866.

(Above) Grace Church; (Top Right) Wedding portrait of Tom Thumb and Lavinia Warren.

053. GRACE CHURCH
802 Broadway at East 10th Street. Hours and general information: www.gracechurchnyc.org or (212) 254-2000

If the saddest ceremony conducted during New York's Civil War era was Lincoln's funeral, the happiest was the marriage of Gen. Tom Thumb to Miss Lavinia Warren. Officiated by the Reverend Thomas Taylor, the ceremony was held here at Grace Church on February 10, 1863. Just when America needed some relief from the war, P. T. Barnum offered up this media event: he dubbed it "The Diamond Wedding"; provided tiny coaches drawn by ponies; and even produced a jealous rival for his superstar dwarf, the equally small Commodore Nutt, to serve as best man.

Jammed into the church were 1,500 people, including every important dignitary in the city—even Gen. Ambrose L. Burnside was able to get away from the fighting long enough to attend. Scalpers sold tickets for as much as $50 each. Tens of thousands more lined Broadway trying to catch a glimpse of the diminutive yet happy couple. This was considered the "wedding of the century," and even the Lincolns joined in the celebration by hosting the newlyweds with a reception at the White House when their honeymoon took them to Washington. It was all in good fun and served to distract the country from the grim reality of war for a few days.

054. ST. DENIS HOTEL
Southwest corner of Broadway and East 11th Street

Although the building has since been stripped of all its architectural detail, in its day the St. Denis was one of the handsomest hotels in the city. Containing over 150 rooms, it was designed in 1851–52 by architect James Renwick, Jr. (1818–1895), who had just completed Grace Church across the street. He would soon move uptown to begin work on his masterpiece, the new St. Patrick's Cathedral. Both Abraham Lincoln and P. T. Barnum are said to have stayed at the St. Denis, and years later Alexander Graham Bell would demonstrate the very first telephone to New Yorkers here in 1877. As one of the best hotels in the city, it was among those set ablaze by the Confederate conspirators Martin and Headley in 1864.

St. Denis building.

IV. Greenwich Village

055. CLARKSON AND CARMINE STREETS
Corner of Clarkson and Varick Streets, at the foot of Seventh Avenue South

As the Civil War dragged on, enlistments in the army dwindled, so President Lincoln imposed a draft on able-bodied men. But many poor whites were outraged to learn that any man wealthy enough could buy his way out of the draft for $300. They also feared that freeing all the slaves in the South would create competition for already scarce jobs. These factors contributed to the rebellion of nearly 50,000 enraged residents of the city's worst slums during July 1863. Racist mobs roamed the city looking for black people to beat, rob, and murder. More than a hundred people were killed during the rioting—not one of the proudest moments in New York City history.

At the time, Seventh Avenue had not yet been cut through the buildings that stood north of Varick Street, so Carmine joined with Clarkson Street in a dogleg at this point. On a lot on the north side of the street, in the middle of the current intersection, stood a Presbyterian Church and a park. It was here, on the night of July 13, that rioters grabbed William Jones, a poor black man who had ventured out to buy some bread. Believing all blacks to be the source of their problems, the mob lynched him from one of the trees in the park. The killers then built a bonfire underneath his body and proceeded to dance a jig around it.

Tradition has it that the residents of an old building that once stood at 92 Grove Street sheltered many black refugees from the thugs during the worst of the rioting, thereby saving their lives. The only hospital willing to help African-Americans during the riots was the Jews Hospital, then at 158 West 28th Street. Later it would change its name to Mt. Sinai Hospital and move uptown to its present location.

New York City Draft riot, 1863: "The rioters burning the
Colored Orphan Asylum at 5th Ave. & 46th St."

Harper's Pictorial History

056. SHERIDAN SQUARE
Christopher Park and nearby Sheridan Square, at the intersection of Seventh Avenue and West 4th Street

General Philip Henry Sheridan (1831–1888) is widely considered one of the Civil War's greatest military leaders. On October 19, 1936, a life-size statue was dedicated here to his memory. The bronze figure was created by Joseph P. Pollia (1893–1954) and paid for by the Grand Army of the Republic and the General Sheridan Memorial Association. It shows Sheridan wearing boots and spurs, but without the horse you would expect in a portrayal of a cavalry officer. Sheridan was

Statue of General Philip Sheridan.

born in Albany, New York, in 1831 and spent nearly his entire life in the Army. However, it wasn't until midway through the Civil War that he began to distinguish himself as an able commander, thereafter becoming one of Grant's favorite generals. He distinguished himself at the battle of Chattanooga, the Overland campaign, the Shenandoah campaign, and ultimately at Appomattox. Grant wrote, "I believe General Sheridan has no superior as a general, either living or dead, and perhaps not an equal." Many New Yorkers like to win bets by knowing that the statue of Sheridan is not in Sheridan Square but in Christopher Park; Sheridan Square, named in honor of the general in 1896, is the smaller, triangular piece of property just to the south and east.

Behind the statue of Sheridan, at the apex of Christopher Park, is a flagstaff raised in 1936 (as was Sheridan's statue) in memory of Elmer Ellsworth and his fire Zouaves. The flagpole was erected to honor Ellsworth as the first commissioned officer to be killed in the Civil War.

057. GENERAL DANIEL SICKLES' HOME
23 Fifth Avenue, northeast corner of Fifth Avenue and East 9th Street

One of the most controversial generals of the Civil War was Daniel Edgar Sickles (1819–1914). He proclaimed himself "The Hero of Gettysburg," but some students of the battle believe that his insubordination, which led to the decimation of his troops, could have lost the war for the Union. There was no more colorful character in mid-nineteenth century America than Dan Sickles. In 1857, he was elected to the U.S. House of Representatives as a Tammany Hall

Home of General Daniel Sickles.

Democrat in favor of maintaining the institution of slavery in the South. Throughout his life he was involved in many scandals, not the least of which was the murder of Philip Barton Key, the son of Francis Scott Key. Although Sickles was a notorious womanizer and philanderer, he took exception when Key had an affair with Sickles' own young wife Teresa. He shot him to death in Washington's Lafayette Park, just across the street from the White House. He was tried in 1859 but was acquitted, the first person to ever be found innocent by reason of temporary insanity. After his release, he returned to live with Teresa in their country home on the Upper West Side, near the corner of 91st Street and Riverside Drive.

General Daniel Sickles.

Then in 1861, when the country was plunged into civil war, Sickles and Col. William Wiley—also a Tammany Hall politician—decided to form their own regiment. They named it Excelsior after the one-word New York State motto. General Sickles commanded the Excelsior Brigade during the Peninsula Campaign, Chancellorsville, and finally Gettysburg. It was there, on July 2, 1863, that Sickles broke the Union line and advanced his men forward against the orders of commanding general George Meade. He took a position in the peach orchard and wheat field nearly a half mile in front of the rest of the Union forces—and suffered tremendous casualties. The maneuver so baffled General Lee that it disrupted his plans to take Little Round Top. Lee couldn't believe that any officer would advance his position so far beyond his own lines without support from other troops, so the Confederates prepared for a large assault—one that never came. Thus they missed the opportunity to seize the higher ground that Little Round Top represented. During the fighting, Sickles himself was hit in the leg by a cannon ball and carried off the field on a stretcher. Following the amputation of his leg, he sent the fractured bone to the Army Medical Museum, where it became a great tourist attraction; it is on display in the National Museum of Health and Medicine to this day. For his courage and gallantry under fire, Sickles was awarded the Medal of Honor in 1897.

After the war, General Sickles returned to New York and bought a townhouse at 23 Fifth Avenue, on the northeast corner of East 9th Street, where he lived until his death in 1914 at the age of 94. Even in old age, Sickles continued to be controversial. While serving as ambassador to Spain from 1867–1874 he engaged in several affairs with well-known women, including Isabella, the former queen. He was re-elected to Congress (1893–1895); still later he was appointed to head the New York Commission for Gettysburg Monuments, during which tenure the commission discovered that Sickles had "misplaced" $27,000.

058. TENTH STREET STUDIO AND DANIEL CHESTER FRENCH HOUSE
45-51 West 10th Street and 58 West 10th Street

In 1856, the well-known architect Richard Morris Hunt built the Tenth Street Studio that stood here until 1959, now replaced by an apartment house. The old building contained nearly two dozen combination studio/living spaces for some of America's greatest artists. Those studios were designed so that all the residents had perfect light for working. The roster of artists who rented space here reads like a *Who's Who of American Artists*: William Merritt Chase, Augustus Saint-Gaudens, Winslow Homer, Eastman Johnson, John LaFarge, and Emanuel Leutze (most famous for his historical painting of *Washington Crossing the Delaware*) all worked on Civil War commissions in this building. Winslow Homer, who became well-known for his sketches from the battlefront in the Civil War, had a studio here during the 1870s, and said it was much more than just a place to work. He felt that the cooperative spirit of the building fostered an "atmosphere of comradeship" among the artists. In 1863, Edwin Booth, the great Shakespearean actor and brother of John Wilkes Booth, came here to pose for his friend Launt Thompson.

Tenth Street Studio.

Thompson's bronze bust of Booth in the role of Hamlet is now displayed at The Players on Gramercy Park.

One of the few major artists of the era who did not work at the Tenth Street Studio had his own studio nearby. Daniel Chester French (1850–1931), the artist who sculpted the immense seated Lincoln for the Lincoln Memorial in Washington, had his own work space at 58 West 10th Street, the current site of NYU's Creative Writing Program. From 1914–1922, French worked on that statue here and at Chesterwood, his summer home in the Berkshires in western Massachusetts. In addition to this and other Lincoln statues commissioned from him, French sculpted figures of Commodore George H. Perkins, General Russell Alger, Gen. Ulysses S. Grant, and Gen. Joseph Hooker, to name only a few.

059. WINFIELD SCOTT HOUSE
24 West 12th Street. General information: (212) 998-8739.

General Winfield Scott.

When the first shots were fired on Fort Sumter in 1861, the commanding general of the United States Army was Lt. Gen. Winfield Scott. People had long considered him the ablest commander in U.S. history, but by the time the war began he was 74 years old and well past his prime. He had the distinction of serving on active duty longer than any other general. He was a veteran of the War of 1812 and the Mexican American War, and had been the unsuccessful Whig party candidate for president in 1852. On April 20, 1853, Scott purchased this new house for $26,000 and remained here for the duration of the Civil War. General Scott was aware that he was no longer able to command an army in the field; at 300 pounds he was said to be too large to even mount his own horse. In April 1861, he offered command of the entire army to his best young officer, Col. Robert E. Lee of Virginia, but Lee turned him down. That very same day Virginia seceded from the Union and Lee accepted the command of troops in his home state. Ironically, Scott was also a native Virginian, but chose to remain loyal to the Federal government. General Irvin McDowell was given field command of the Union army, only to be defeated at the first battle of Bull Run that July. On November 1, 1861, Gen. George B. McClellan forced Scott's resignation from the army when McClellan assumed command. General Scott's initial plan to prosecute the war in the South was called the Anaconda Plan. It proposed a long, drawn-out strangulation of the Confederacy through a blockade of its ports and a Union seizure of the Mississippi River. Members of the press mocked his strategy, since they believed the South would be defeated quickly on the battlefield; but four years later Scott's plan brought Union victory. Upon the elderly general's retirement, Lincoln acknowledged Scott's loyalty in a message to Congress that noted "how faithfully, ably and brilliantly he has served the country." When General Scott passed

Home of General Winfield Scott.

away in 1866, he had served his country for a total of 53 years. Today the interior of General Scott's home has been converted into offices and classrooms for NYU's Italian Language Department. Often the school mounts exhibitions on the ground floor, and it is worth stopping in to view the space and small garden in back. A commemorative plaque is affixed to the beautifully preserved exterior of the building noting that it is now on the National Register of Historic Places.

060. MACY'S
East side of Sixth Avenue just below West 14th Street

Macy's, New York's most famous department store, was founded in Haverhill, Massachusetts, in 1851. In 1858, Rowland Hussey Macy moved to New York and opened a new store named R. H. Macy Dry Goods at 204-206 Sixth Avenue. The numbering system on Sixth Avenue has been changed, but 204-206 would have been in a building that no longer exists on the east side of the street just below West 14th Street, now replaced by a larger office building. As the business grew, Macy's expanded into neighboring storefronts until R. H. Macy relocated the enterprise to its current site at Herald Square in 1902. During the Civil War, Macy's, like many other retailers, did a brisk business selling uniforms and supplies to the troops. The company produced Zouave jackets, capes, and toiletries, and even shipped them to soldiers in the field.

Macy's during the 1800s.

061. PALACE GARDEN
On the north side of West 14th Street between Sixth and Seventh Avenues

Colonel Ellsworth's New York Fire Zouaves.

The Palace Garden was one of a number of private outdoor green spaces in the city used for various functions, including fairs, rallies, and open-air meetings. During the Civil War, the Palace Garden on West 14th Street was located approximately where the McBurney Branch of the YMCA stands today. It was used as an assembly point for recruits. Here the 11th Regiment, also known as the 1st Fire Zouaves, unanimously elected Elmer Ellsworth as their colonel. Ellsworth would become the first officer killed during the war. Temporary barracks were built here, but they were particularly filthy, according to contemporary accounts, so most of the officers returned to their homes at night—leaving the enlisted men free to roam the nearby saloons and get into trouble. The Zouaves adopted the most colorful uniforms of the war: they sported billowing red Arabian-looking pants, tunics with sashes, and brightly colored turbans. Although the regiment fought at first Bull Run, many soldiers deserted after the battle and returned to New York.

062. DELAMATER IRON WORKS
West of 10th Avenue between West 13th and West 14th Streets

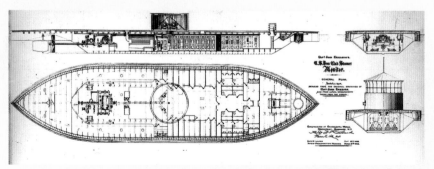

Plans for the USS *Monitor*.

Before this area became a meat-packing district, it was devoted to heavy industry, with mills and factories producing everything from plaster to pianos. One full block along Tenth Avenue (where 51 Tenth Avenue stands today) was the site of the Delamater Iron Works. Cornelius H. Delamater (1821–1889) was a partner of the naval architect John Ericsson, and here they developed the modern screw propeller that changed ocean travel forever. In 1861, Ericsson commissioned Delamater to fabricate an engine to drive the first ironclad, the USS *Monitor*, and later the even larger 320-foot *Dictator*. At one time there was a plaque here to commemorate their achievements, but it has disappeared along with all vestiges of the iron industry in New York City. Delamater's summer estate still stands on Long Island in the village of Asharoken.

Battle between the *Monitor* and *Merrimack*.

V. Union Square to Madison Square

063. 9th REGIMENT TABLET
Southeast corner of East 13th Street and University Place

On Memorial Day 1908, this tablet was unveiled to mark the former headquarters of the 9th Regiment. The old two-story building just south of Union Square has been replaced by an office building. Forty-seven years before the unveiling, on May 27, 1861, 850 members of the regiment marched off from this point to join the Army of the Potomac. The 9th arrived in Washington on

Ninth Regiment historical marker.

June 8, 1861, and was mustered in as the 83rd New York for the duration of the war, seeing action at Bull Run, South Mountain, Antietam, Fredericksburg, Chancellorsville, Gettysburg, the Wilderness, Spotsylvania, and Cold Harbor. The plaque notes: "They returned home June 11, 1864, with 17 officers and 78 enlisted men after having gone through 24 battles." In between, 379 men were killed and the rest wounded. This was typical of the efforts and sacrifices made by New York volunteers during the war.

064. WALLACK'S THEATER
842-846 Broadway, on the northeast corner of East 13th Street

Wallack's Theater building in the later 1800s.

In September 1861, John Lester Wallack (1820–1888) opened the second Wallack's Theatre at Broadway and East 13th Street, now replaced by a modern multiplex cinema. As New York's affluent citizens moved further north, so did the stores and entertainment facilities that catered to them. Wallack's new theater was designed to be the most elegant in the city, with ticket prices ranging from a quarter to as much as several dollars for the best seats. Wallack's inaugural play here was a three-act drama entitled *The New President*. Of particular Civil War interest was the New York debut of actor John Wilkes Booth as *Richard III*. Booth came from a family of actors, but his performances from March 17 through April 5, 1862, received less-than-stellar reviews. His mediocre acting ability was always compared to that of his brother Edwin, widely considered the greatest Shakespearean actor in America.

065. MAYOR C. GODFREY GUNTHER RESIDENCE
239 East 14th Street

The third and last of New York's Civil War mayors was C. Godfrey Gunther (1822–1885), who served from 1864–1866. During his administration he lived at what was then 145 East 14th Street, a building west of Second Avenue on the north side of the street that has been greatly renovated since Gunther's day. The street numbering system has been changed, so that today 145 is the building at 239 East 14th. In 1863, city voters, unhappy with the Republican administration of George Opdyke (1805–1880), replaced him with Gunther, a Copperhead Democrat. Copperheads were officially called Peace Democrats, but Republicans compared them to the poisonous copperhead snake and the name stuck. Copperheads were Northerners who opposed the war and hoped to make a peaceful settlement with the South by agreeing to allow slavery to continue. Gunther was much less sympathetic to Abraham Lincoln's policies than Opdyke, especially on the issue of emancipation.

John Gunther.

Gunther, the son of immigrants, was a life-long New Yorker and very popular with the German community that dominated this neighborhood during mid-century. Godfrey joined his father's successful fur business and was a member of one of the city's politically active volunteer fire departments, the Eagle Hose Company No. 1. After having used both his wealth and political affiliations to win election, he served as mayor for only one term. It was during Gunther's tenure that Confederate terrorists attempted to burn down the city. The Southerners mistakenly believed that if they mounted an arson attack on New York the Copperheads would rise up and rebel against the Union, but the attack only caused more people to side against them.

During his administration, Gunther did all he could to stop the war and end hostilities, so he was not comforted by Northern victories. As mayor in 1864, he vetoed plans to celebrate Sherman's taking of Atlanta and Sheridan's victories in the Shenandoah Valley. As an outspoken opponent of Lincoln and his abolitionist policy, when the martyred president's funeral cortege passed through New York City in 1865, Gunther vetoed the publication of tributes delivered in honor of Lincoln. The Common Council overrode his veto, however, and published *The Obsequies of Abraham Lincoln* against the mayor's wishes.

066. ACADEMY OF MUSIC
Northeast corner of East 14th Street and Irving Place

From 1854–1886, the Academy of Music stood where the Con Ed Building is located today. It boasted the largest auditorium in the city during the war years, seating more than 4,000 people. In addition to cultural events, it hosted large political and civic gatherings as well. On July 4, 1863, New York's Gov. Horatio Seymour (1810–1886) spoke to a full house at the Academy. Although a Union supporter, he believed that Lincoln's efforts to free the slaves violated democratic principles and trampled on the rights of southern states. "Remember this, that the bloody, and treasonable, and revolutionary doctrine of public necessity can be proclaimed by a mob as well as by a Government." These words from his speech were poorly timed, because a week later the Draft Riots erupted, during which mobs terrorized the city for several bloody days.

Governor Horatio Seymour.

Other events were not as incendiary. Edward Everett (1794–1865) of Massachusetts spoke at the Academy of Music one day, holding the audience spellbound for several hours; Everett was the great orator who spoke for two hours at Gettysburg before Lincoln delivered his two-minute Gettysburg Address. Lincoln himself visited the Academy of Music in February 1861 as president-elect to attend a performance of Verdi's opera, *Un Ballo In Maschera* (*A Masked Ball*). Later, in April of the same year, Walt Whitman attended that same opera, and as he left the theater he heard the newsboys shouting that Fort Sumter had been attacked.

The Great Russian Ball at the Academy of Music, 1863.

067. UNION SQUARE
Broadway and East 14th Street

For nearly two centuries, Union Square has been the site of historic demonstrations and political rallies on a giant scale. During the Civil War, it was the site of many protests, speeches, and parades. On April 20, 1861, a mass rally held here supported Lincoln's call for 75,000 volunteers. A crowd estimated at 100,000 to 250,000 people turned out to listen to the 20 dignitaries scheduled to speak that day. The highlight was the appearance of the Union officer who had been in command of Fort Sumter, Maj. Robert Anderson (1805–1871). Following his surrender on April 13, 1861, he and his men had been allowed to return north aboard the *Baltic*, arriving in New York harbor on April 19. Although a Southerner by birth and pro-slavery himself, Anderson remained loyal to the Union. He was promoted to brigadier general and became the North's first national hero. The flag that had flown over Fort Sumter was draped over the equestrian statue of George Washington at the south end of the square. The crowd that wildly cheered Anderson that day was the largest ever assembled in the country, and the *New York Tribune* reported it as "the greatest popular demonstration ever known in America."

(Top left) Major Robert Anderson; (Above) Rally in Union Square, April 20, 1861.

Throughout the war other large rallies were held in Union Square. Most were intended to bolster the morale of the people of New York, because each new defeat made it seem that the war would never end. When Gen. George McClellan ran for president in 1864, the custom was that candidates did not make their own campaign speeches, so Robert Winthrop of Massachusetts, a former speaker of the U.S. House of Representatives, spoke to a large crowd here on McClellan's behalf. On election day, McClellan carried the city against Lincoln but failed to win the state. Also in 1864, the women of the Sanitary Commission hosted a giant charity bazaar called the Metropolitan Sanitary Fair in the square, and in only three weeks raised somewhere between $500,000– $1,000,000 for medical supplies for the troops.

It was also in Union Square on March 5, 1864, that the Union League Club presented the colors to the North's first black regiment, the 20th U.S. Colored Troops. Oddly enough, during the early years of the war the South used the services of black men but the North did not. Eventually a group of white citizens, many members of the Union League Club, formed the New York Association for Colored Volunteers and outfitted them. Their standard was emblazoned with the slogan "Rather Die a Free Man Than Live To Be a Slave."

On April 25, 1865, following Lincoln's death, a massive ecumenical outdoor service was held in the square for the assassinated president. Archbishop John McCloskey, Rabbi Samuel Isaacs, and Reverend Stephen Tyng led the worshippers. This was the last grand rally of the Civil War era.

068. ABRAHAM LINCOLN STATUE
Union Square

Soon after the death of Lincoln, the Union League Club commissioned sculptor Henry Kirke Brown (1814–1886) to create a monument in honor of the slain president. When this memorial was dedicated in Union Square on September 16, 1870, it became the first outdoor statue of Lincoln in America. Originally the statue was surrounded by a fence that bore an inscription of Lincoln's famous words, "With malice toward none; with charity toward all," but the fence disappeared some unknown time later. Shortly after finishing this work, Brown made another statue of Lincoln for Brooklyn's Prospect Park, and since then hundreds of memorials to Lincoln have been dedicated in towns across America.

Statue of Abraham Lincoln, ca. 1909.

069. MAYOR GEORGE OPDYKE RESIDENCE
79 Fifth Avenue, at the time midway between East 15th and East 16th Streets

Major George Opdyke.

In 1862, when the Democrats split ranks, Democratic mayor Fernando Wood was replaced by the Republican millionaire merchant George Opdyke. During his single term as mayor, Opdyke worked to raise troops and promote economic stability in the city. At the time he lived at 79 Fifth Avenue, but the street numbering system has changed since those days and his home has been replaced by a tall office building.

Before the war, Opdyke made his fortune by manufacturing and selling clothing, much of it intended for the Southern markets. As soon as war broke out he switched over to manufacturing uniforms and blankets for the troops—and began to do even better. As clothing inspector for the army, it was Opdyke who approved the use of shoddy material by Brooks Brothers. He also ran a rifle factory manufacturing carbines that he sold to the government at inflated prices. During the Draft Riots of 1863, the mob failed in its attempt to burn down his home but did destroy the gun factory.

Opdyke was pro-Union but had supported Salmon P. Chase in his 1860 bid against Lincoln for the presidential nomination. Opdyke and Lincoln did not get along, and when Opdyke tried to bully Lincoln into removing William Seward from his position as secretary of state the president lost his temper. As a result, Opdyke refused to back Lincoln during the 1864 presidential campaign. The Draft Riots killed any hope Opdyke himself had for re-election in 1864, and he was replaced by the Democrat Godfrey Gunther. In 1880, Opdyke died at his home, then at 1 East 47th Street.

070. THE PLAYERS and EDWIN BOOTH STATUE
16 Gramercy Park South and Gramercy Park, between 20th and 21st Streets.
General information: www.theplayersnyc.org or (212) 475-6116.

Throughout the Civil War, Edwin Booth was known by everyone in America as one of the greatest Shakespearean actors in the world. But after the assassination of President Lincoln in 1865, he became known as the brother of John Wilkes Booth. Their father Junius Brutus Booth (1796–1852) had been an acclaimed actor, and three of the Booth children followed in his footsteps. Until their father's death in 1852, the family was very close, but there was competitive rivalry between Edwin and his brothers John Wilkes and Junius, Jr. As a result, they appeared on stage together only once. Due to his great theatrical abilities and popularity, Edwin Booth made several fortunes during his lifetime, and in 1888 he used some of that wealth to open a private club he called The Players, still at 16 Gramercy Park. Early members included Mark Twain, Gen. William Sherman, President Grover Cleveland, architect Stanford White, and a host of other prominent men. When White oversaw the club's renovations, he waived his architectural fee in exchange for lifetime membership.

(Top right) Portrait of Edwin Booth as Hamlet.
(Above) The Players.

Inside this private club are many remarkable items. In addition to Edwin Booth's own library containing thousands of theatrical books and papers is Booth's remorseful letter that he addressed to the American people following the assassination. During the last five years of Booth's life he lived on the third floor of The Players, and his apartment has been preserved as it was on June 7, 1893, the day he died. In the lobby of The Players is the bust of Booth sculpted by his friend Launt Thompson in 1863, and in the library is the Hamlet Prize that Edwin received in recognition of his portrayal of Hamlet on stage for 100 consecutive nights. The medal was designed by Louis Comfort Tiffany and presented to him at the Winter Garden Theater in January 1867, with Adm. David G. Farragut, Maj. General Robert Anderson, and other Union army officers in the audience.

Following the death of his wife in 1863, Edwin Booth bought a house at 28 East 19th Street, and his mother and daughter lived there until the time of the assassination. That house, at the location of today's ABC Carpet building, has been torn down. During the Draft Riots of July 1863, the Booths (including John Wilkes, who was visiting at the time) hid a Union officer and his black servant from a bloodthirsty mob that would certainly have brutalized them. Less than two years later, when Edwin discovered that his brother had shot Lincoln, he was grief-stricken. He temporarily retired from acting and lived in isolation in the East 19th Street house with his family. Throughout the war, Edwin Booth had supported the Union and agreed with the concept of emancipation that his brother John Wilkes so strongly opposed.

Most of Booth's adoring fans did not hold the act of his brother against him, although in 1879 a traveling salesman named Mark Gray attempted to shoot Edwin Booth while the latter performed in *Richard II*. He missed, but Booth kept the bullet inside a gold brooch engraved with the words, "From Mark Gray to Edwin Booth, April 23, 1879." Booth lived another decade until 1893, but he was forever overshadowed by the terrible deed of his infamous brother.

In 1918, a life-size statue of Edwin Booth was placed in the middle of Gramercy Park and dedicated to the memory of the great actor. The bronze shows him dressed as Hamlet, his most famous role. The sculptor, Edmond T. Quinn (1868–1929), chose to depict Booth rising from his chair to make the famous soliloquy, "To be, or not to be...." The bronze Booth stands facing the actor's last residence, The Players.

071. NATIONAL ARTS CLUB
15 Gramercy Park South. General information: www.nationalartsclub.org or (212) 475-3424.

Next door to The Players today is the National Arts Club, once the home of Samuel Tilden (1814–1886). In 1859, Tilden supported a congressional resolution to attempt a compromise with the South. It would have authorized the United States to purchase Cuba from Spain for the sole purpose of annexing it as a slave state, but it failed passage. During the Civil War, Tilden supported the Union but did not care for Lincoln, so he played no significant role. In 1876, the wealthy Tilden was the Democratic candidate for president; he won America's popular vote but lost in the electoral college to Republican Rutherford B. Hayes. Today a statue of Tilden stands on Riverside Drive at West 112th Street.

072. THEODORE ROOSEVELT BIRTHPLACE NATIONAL HISTORIC SITE
28 East 20th Street. Hours: T–Sat 9:00 a.m. – 5:00 p.m. General information: www.nps.gov/thrb or (212) 260-1616. Admission charge.

If you have ever wondered what a Civil War-era home might have looked like, the Theodore Roosevelt (1858–1919) Birthplace is the place to visit. Roosevelt was only three years old when the Civil War began, so he played no part in its history, but his birthplace is of considerable interest. The home where he lived from 1858–1872 captures a moment in the lives of wealthy New Yorkers during the mid-nineteenth century. In 1861, it was Theodore Roosevelt, Sr., Teddy's father, along with William E. Dodge and Theodore Bronson, who lobbied Congress to pass the Allotment Act of 1861 that allowed the army to send soldiers' pay directly to their families. Until then many soldiers had fallen prey to gamblers, prostitutes, and thieves, spending and drinking up most of their money while their families back home went hungry.

It is also interesting to note that Theodore Roosevelt's father bought his way out of the 1863 draft. Since his wife was from Georgia and a supporter of the Confederacy, he may have wanted to avoid a conflict between family members, but later this was a source of embarrassment for his son,

National Arts Club.

the future president. Although the building was demolished in 1916, Roosevelt's death in 1919 reminded Americans that they had lost an important part of their history, so in 1923 the building and its interior were meticulously recreated to their 1865 appearance and opened as a museum. The edifice is an exact replica of what a fashionable New York brownstone would have looked like during the Civil War. Theodate Pope Riddle, one of the first female architects in America, oversaw the project.

Theodore Roosevelt Birthplace National Historic Site.

073. ARMS FACTORY and UNION STEAM WORKS
Northeast corner of Second Avenue and East 21st Street; and Second Avenue and East 22nd Street

Once a weapons factory stood on the northeast corner of Second Avenue and East 21st Street, which locals called the Armory. It was owned by George W. Farlee, Mayor Opdyke's son-in-law, who let out the upper floors as a drill room for local militia. After the Draft Riot mob burned the Ninth District draft office, the rioters decided to raid the armory to commandeer needed weapons. At the time nearly a thousand serviceable rifles were stored here awaiting shipment to the troops in the field, and officials were justly worried about them falling into the wrong hands;

Burning of the Second Avenue Armory, July 1863.

until then the rioters had been armed only with clubs and paving stones. The police department had only 34 men available to protect the armory, but for a while that small force was enough to hold off the attackers. As the crowd grew to overwhelming numbers, the police decided to abandon the armory and the rioters seized the building. After "liberating" many of the weapons, some in the mob set the armory on fire—without worrying about their own people still inside. Thirteen rioters were killed when they became trapped on the upper floors of the burning building.

The Draft Riot mob learned of another cache of weapons stored at the Union Steam Works on Second Avenue, a block from the Armory. The small squad of policemen assigned to secure that building was in danger of being overrun by thousands of rioters when Capt. John Helme and six platoons of additional policemen arrived on the scene. After a bloody battle waged in the streets outside, the police managed to clear the building. They then shifted the rifles into a wagon and attempted to carry them away to safety. But first they had to slowly fight their way through the crowd down 22nd Street to First Avenue. At that point they fired several volleys into the mob, which finally dispersed. This was the most intense fighting during the riots. In retaliation, the mob returned to the abandoned steam works and set them on fire. Neither building has survived.

074. STEPHEN CRANE RESIDENCE
143 East 23rd Street

Stephen Crane.

Although he lived a relatively short life, author Stephen Crane (1871–1900) wrote many books and articles, one of which became perhaps the most famous novel on a Civil War theme, *The Red Badge of Courage*. It was the first book about the conflict that focused on the emotions of the soldiers instead of their accomplishments. Crane was born in Newark, New Jersey, but as an adult spent a good deal of time in New York frequenting the saloons, dance halls, and brothels along the Bowery. He claimed that he did this to perform research for books such as *Maggie: A Girl of the Streets*, but the squalid lifestyle appealed to him—and took a toll on his health. He struggled to make a living in the city from 1893–1895 and lived wherever he could find cheap accommodations. For a while that was with three friends, one the artist R. G. Vosburgh, at 143 West 23rd Street in a building replaced in 1927 by the larger Hotel Kenmore at 145 East 23rd Street, where he researched a series of sketches for the *New York Journal*. Then in 1893 he met the artist Corwin Knapp Linson, who had a studio on West 30th Street and Broadway. While sitting for a portrait by Linson, Crane read several articles about the Civil War in *Century* magazine and began to write *The Red Badge of Courage*. It was originally published in 1894 in serial form in a half dozen newspapers and immediately brought him fame. Unfortunately, his life of excess contributed to his early death from tuberculosis at 28.

075. UNION CLUB and UNION LEAGUE CLUB
160 Fifth Avenue at West 21st Street; and 26 East 17th Street, near Broadway facing on Union Square

The clubhouse for the Union Club, founded in 1836, stood on the northwest corner of Fifth Avenue and West 21st Street from 1855–1903. The club was the second oldest private club in the country and counted among its members the wealthiest and most powerful men in the city. John Ericsson, U. S. Grant, Winfield Scott, Philip Sheridan, and William Tecumseh Sherman were all members. When war was declared, the club board refused to expel member Judah P. Benjamin (1811–1884), who was U.S. senator from Louisiana and had been appointed first attorney general of the Confederacy; instead, the board allowed Benjamin to resign quietly, which upset many of the more militant Unionists.

Another member, the Democratic millionaire August Belmont, was a Copperhead who backed Stephen A. Douglas for the presidency and lobbied for Southern concessions right up to the attack on Fort Sumter. With the outbreak of hostilities, Belmont dropped his support of the South and helped Republican Congressman Francis Blair of Pennsylvania raise a German-American regiment for the Union. Still, Belmont's less than one hundred percent support of Lincoln and the Union was more than some patriotic members of the club could take.

Union League Club, East 17th Street.

Led by four members, Henry Adams Bellows, Frederick Law Olmsted, George Templeton Strong, and Oliver Wolcott Gibbs, a large contingent broke away and formed the Union League Club.

In February 1863, 66 members established the new club, and within months it had 350 members, most former members of the Union Club. Their primary goal was to do all they could to preserve the Union. Shortly after the Union League Club was founded, the Draft Riots broke out in the city, during which club members saved their building by barricading themselves into the clubhouse at 26 East 17th Street. In the riots' aftermath, to show they were not intimidated by the anti-Union factions that had rampaged across the city, they sponsored the first black infantry regiment to serve in the Union army. A thousand black men who had volunteered for service in the 20th Regiment U.S. Colored Troops passed in review in front of the clubhouse on Union Square on March 5, 1864. They marched with muskets and fixed bayonets down Broadway to troopships waiting to take them to New Orleans. After the war, the Union League Club helped fund a number of projects, including the placement of the statue of Abraham Lincoln in Union Square and the construction of the Statue of Liberty in New York Harbor.

076. GENERAL JOHN DIX RESIDENCE
3 West 21st Street

Major General John Adams Dix (1798–1879), a lifelong New York politician, lived at 3 West 21st Street in a house similar to the one that still stands next door at 5 West 21st Street. When Maj. Robert Anderson returned to New York following his surrender of Fort Sumter in April 1861, John Dix hosted a reception for him at his home and invited a hundred of the city's most prominent citizens to meet the now-famous soldier. Mayors, governors, and religious leaders all crowded into his parlor to honor the Union's first hero. Dix, himself a former senator as well as

Union Club on the corner and house of General Dix next door, ca. 1893.

former secretary of the treasury, had just volunteered for active service even though he was a staunch Democrat and had supported presidential candidate Stephen Douglas against Lincoln. In spite of their strained relationship, Lincoln appointed Dix to the rank of major general and was soon rewarded when General Dix arrested the Maryland legislature so the members could not vote on secession from the Union. It was also Dix who finally quelled the draft rioters in 1863 and who warned the city about the Confederate arson attack in 1864. Since he was considered too old for field command, he was appointed to head the Army's Department of the East and was headquartered in New York City for most of the war. It was Dix who brokered an exchange of prisoners with the Confederacy that became known as the Dix-Hill Cartel. Fort Dix, New Jersey, is named in his honor.

General John A. Dix.

077. SAMUEL F. B. MORSE RESIDENCE
5 West 22nd Street

Samuel F. B. Morse, the inventor of the telegraph who was an artist as well, lived at 5 West 22nd Street in a house no longer standing. He was 70 years old at the outbreak of the Civil War, much too old to take an active part, but since the 1850s he had been known as a defender of slavery. Morse considered slavery to be sanctioned by God and wrote a treatise on the subject called *An Argument on the Ethical Position of Slavery*. "My creed on the subject of slavery is short," he wrote. "Slavery per se is not sin. It is a social condition ordained from the beginning of the world for the wisest purposes, benevolent and disciplinary, by Divine Wisdom." He also believed that the Pope was a despot of the worst sort, intent on helping Catholics take over America. Fortunately for Morse, he is remembered more for his inventions and his beautiful paintings than for his social theories. At one time a marker commemorated the site of his home here. There is also a statue of Morse in Central Park and his tomb is in Brooklyn's Green-Wood Cemetery.

Samuel Morse.

078. BOOTH THEATRE
Southeast corner of Sixth Avenue and West 23rd Street

In 1868, Edwin Booth—still recovering from his grief over the actions of his brother John Wilkes Booth—realized his dream to build his own theater in New York. When it opened the following year, the Booth name was again praised instead of reviled. The state-of-the-art Booth Theatre seated 1,800 people and employed the most modern stage equipment, lighting, and accoutrements available. It stood on the southeast corner of Sixth Avenue and 23rd Street until 1874, when it was forced to close during the national economic recession. A bust of Edwin Booth and a tablet marking the site of his theater were placed here, but those have disappeared to urban development. The new building on site, called "The Caroline," has placed a plaque on the Sixth Avenue side of the building relating some of the history of this location.

(Top left) Booth Theater historical marker;
(Above) Booth Theater.

079. WILLIAM H. SEWARD MONUMENT
Madison Square, near the corner at East 23rd Street and Broadway

In 1876, sculptor Randolph Rogers (1825-1892) unveiled his larger-than-life bronze statue of William H. Seward in Madison Square. Seward was Lincoln's powerful secretary of state and had been both a senator from and governor of New York before the war. He was a prominent abolitionist and had fought Lincoln for the 1860 Republican presidential nomination. Many people remember Seward for his purchase of Alaska from Russia for $7.2 million, which at the time was considered "Seward's Folly." Many guidebooks have mistakenly reported that Rogers put Seward's head on a body of Lincoln he had sculpted earlier.

Statue of William Seward.

080. ADMIRAL DAVID FARRAGUT MONUMENT
Madison Square, near East 26th Street

Admiral David Farragut monument.

One of the most perfectly executed public memorials in the city is the statue of Admiral David Farragut (1801–1870), also located in Madison Square. In 1881, Augustus Saint-Gaudens placed his statue here on a pedestal designed by the noted architect Stanford White. In this case, the black granite pedestal is nearly as interesting as the sculpture it supports. The figure shows Farragut standing in the wind on his ship's prow, ready to give the command "Damn the torpedoes! Full speed ahead!" This order would help Farragut win the battle of Mobile Bay and make him the Civil War's most famous naval officer. Three members of the crew of Farragut's ship *Hartford* took part in the memorial's unveiling. A neighborhood in east central Brooklyn was named for Farragut as well. This bronze composition was Saint-Gaudens' first public commission and helped establish him as the country's foremost sculptor. As a tribute to Saint-Gaudens himself, a nearby playground on Second Avenue at East 20th Street has been named in his honor.

081. CHESTER A. ARTHUR MONUMENT
Madison Square, near East 26th Street

Although this memorial by sculptor George Edwin Bissell (1839–1920) honors Chester A. Arthur (1829-1886) as the 21st president, it should also be noted that Arthur held the title of brigadier general during the war and lived nearby on Lexington Avenue. Having been a lawyer specializing in civil rights cases before the war, he served his country in various noncombatant positions throughout the war. Even before war was declared, Arthur had been appointed engineer in chief of the state militia. In 1862, he was promoted inspector general of the state militia, then after a few months quartermaster general. In this capacity it was Arthur's job to provide 15,000 fresh recruits with clothing, blankets, and weapons during the first year of the war. After the war, he returned to his law practice and became more involved in politics. Arthur was sworn in as the 21st president on September 19, 1881, following President Garfield's assassination.

Statue of Chester Arthur.

082. ROSCOE CONKLING MEMORIAL
Madison Square, near the corner at East 23rd Street and Madison Avenue

Statue of Roscoe Conkling.

The statue of Roscoe Conkling (1829–1888) in Madison Square was unveiled by sculptor John Quincy Adams Ward in 1893. It is a larger-than-life bronze statue on a simple granite base. Ward had been offered the commission for the Admiral Farragut memorial in the same park but did not accept it because he was too busy; instead he suggested that the work go to the young Augustus Saint-Gaudens. The latter had never created a public work before, but it is easy to judge the superior quality of Saint-Gaudens' work by comparing these two memorials in Madison Square.

Roscoe Conkling was a controversial figure during the Reconstruction period. He had served in the House of Representatives during the Civil War before he became a U.S. senator in 1867. While Conkling was serving in 1873, the state of Mississippi elected Blanche Bruce (1841–1898), a black man, to the Senate. It was Senate custom for a state's senior senator to escort a newly elected colleague such as Bruce down the Senate aisle to take his oath of office. But the white senator from Mississippi refused to follow tradition—so Conkling rose to his feet and escorted Bruce himself. At one time there was a public school in Brooklyn named in Senator Bruce's honor.

Conkling died of exposure and pneumonia after he fell on Broadway near East 16th Street during the blizzard of 1888. His body was found there, near Union Square, and his friends preferred that site for this monument. However, although Conkling was a prominent Republican, the park commissioners did not consider him important enough to be honored with a statue in Union Square, which they wanted to reserve for memorials to people on the level of Washington and Lincoln. So they relegated Conkling's statue to Madison Square.

083. FIFTH AVENUE HOTEL
200 Fifth Avenue, between West 23rd and West 24th Streets

The elegant Fifth Avenue Hotel that stood on the northwest corner of Fifth Avenue and West 23rd Street until its demolition in 1908 could accommodate 800 guests. When it opened in 1858, it was a state-of-the-art, six-story, white marble building offering guests one of the city's first elevators, dubbed a "vertical railroad." Every bedroom had a fireplace and many had private bathrooms, unusual at the time. During the Civil War, the hotel was a meeting place for New York's high society, and many elegant dances and functions took place here.

When Lincoln relieved Gen. George McClellan of his command in November 1862 following his failure to pursue the enemy in the wake of the Confederate defeat at Antietam, McClellan took up residence at the Fifth Avenue Hotel. On the day he arrived, the street in front of the hotel was jammed with thousands of people hoping to catch a glimpse of the famous general. He appeared on the hotel's balcony to a roar from the enthusiastic crowd. While awaiting further orders from the Army, he met with Democratic party leaders and decided to run for the presidency against Lincoln. Wealthy supporters even gave him a handsome, fully furnished house on West 31st Street, and from there McClellan ran the campaign that might have unseated Lincoln. At the time it was not considered appropriate for politicians to campaign for themselves, so McClellan made only two public appearances during his entire campaign, one of which was at this hotel. McClellan beat Lincoln in the city, 74,000 votes to 37,000, but lost the state- and nationwide tallies. Following his defeat, McClellan took an extended tour of Europe. Upon his return in 1868, he reviewed a parade of war veterans from the same hotel balcony from which he had campaigned earlier. The crowd spilled out of Madison Square into the surrounding streets, and the revelry is said to have continued well into the night. McClellan stayed in New York for a number of years working as the chief engineer for the Department of Docks. He then founded Geo. B. McClellan

Fifth Avenue Hotel.

and Co., a consulting firm of engineers and accountants, before returning to his home state of New Jersey to become governor.

General Benjamin Butler (1818-1893) established his headquarters at the Fifth Avenue Hotel during the election turmoil in 1864. The city had feared that the Confederates would try to sabotage the election by launching a firebomb attack on the city. The Union sent a strong military presence, which deterred them temporarily; but weeks later, after the troops had left town, the Confederates made good on their threat and set fire to this and a dozen other hotels. Their leader, Lt. Col. Robert Martin, was actually registered at the Fifth Avenue Hotel.

Lincoln's opponents were not the only ones who favored the hotel. General Ulysses S. Grant was the guest of honor at a reception given for him on November 20, 1865, celebrating the end of the war. Whenever he stayed at the hotel, he always reserved rooms 43 and 44, which faced onto West 24th Street. It was at the Fifth Avenue Hotel that the idea of his running for president was born. Edwin

General Benjamin Butler.

Booth and his bride Mary Devlin also lived in a suite at this hotel as newlyweds in 1861, and Gen. William Tecumseh Sherman stayed in a large suite here for two years before he bought a house uptown in 1888.

On the ground floor of the hotel were two shops favored by Abraham Lincoln. One was occupied by the Knox Hat Store. Its proprietors offered the president a new hat free in exchange for his old one, a bargain that the thrifty Lincoln could not refuse. The other store was rented by Maillard Chocolates. Lincoln liked their candies so much that he often served them to guests at the White House.

VI. Midtown

084. CHESTER A. ARTHUR RESIDENCE
123 Lexington Avenue, between East 28th and East 29th Streets

Chester A. Arthur lived at 123 Lexington Avenue in a house that still stands, although the building has been renovated. As an abolitionist and champion of civil rights, Arthur became a Republican and a supporter of Lincoln and his policies. During the Civil War, Arthur was appointed engineer in chief of the state militia, then inspector general of the militia, and eventually quartermaster general. These appointments carried the rank of brigadier general, although he did not see combat during the war. Under President Grant, Arthur was appointed customs collector of the port of New York. Arthur was living here on Lexington Avenue as vice president when he took the presidential oath of office on the night of September 19, 1881, following the assassination of James Garfield. Number 123 was also the site of Arthur's own death in November 1886. In 1964, a group placed a commemorative plaque on the building, which is now displayed in the lobby window.

Home of Chester Arthur today.

085. CHURCH OF THE TRANSFIGURATION, ALSO CALLED "THE LITTLE CHURCH AROUND THE CORNER"

1 East 29th Street, between Fifth and Madison Avenues. Hours and general information: www.littlechurch.org or (212) 684-6770.

"The Little Church Around the Corner" today.

During the 1800s, most Americans considered actors and actresses to be unsavory characters on a par with thieves and prostitutes. When an actor named Joseph Jefferson asked the pastor of a nearby church to conduct a funeral service for fellow actor George Holland, the minister declined, but suggested that he and his friends try "the little church around the corner," noting that they did "that sort of thing." Jefferson retorted, "In that case, sir, God bless the Little Church Around the Corner," and the sobriquet stuck. The first rector of the church, Reverend George H. Houghton (1820–1897), did indeed conduct the ceremony for the actor in question, and the church became a favorite of actors in general. As a result, Edwin Booth was buried from this church. A memorial window created by John LaFarge in Booth's memory depicts him in his role of Hamlet.

During the Draft Riots of 1863, the same Reverend Houghton allowed nearly 300 black people to find safety in his church and adjacent buildings. Although the rioters threatened the church, the brave minister blocked the door wielding a large cross. In the end he managed to talk them out of violence. Another window in the transept memorializes a black couple, George and Elizabeth Wilson, who worked for the church for 30 years following the riots.

086. GENERAL GEORGE B. McCLELLAN RESIDENCE
22 West 31st Street, between Fifth Avenue and Broadway

In 1863, friends and supporters of Gen. George B. McClellan bought a comfortable, four-story brick house for him at 22 West 31st Street, at the time a desirable residential address but long ago replaced by commercial buildings. The Democratic Copperhead factions in the city were eager to court McClellan's favor after President Lincoln replaced him as Union commander. McClellan and his family lived here and enjoyed the social life of the city, attending grand balls and the theater. Frequently he was seen in the company of prominent men, including Governor Horatio Seymour, August Belmont, John Jacob Astor, and Samuel Barlow, all conservative in their politics and opposed to Lincoln's agenda. While in the city, McClellan prepared his final report as commander of the Army of the Potomac, while Lincoln met with General Grant to try to find McClellan a new command. Once McClellan announced his plans to run for president against Lincoln

General George B. McClellan.

in 1864, Lincoln feared that the general's election would lead to a humiliating peace with the South and that all the sacrifices of the war would have been in vain. During the campaign, McClellan spent most of his time at his country home in Orange, New Jersey; only once, on November 5, 1864, did he make a political appearance in New York, on the balcony of the Fifth Avenue Hotel. Although McClellan carried the city in the election, state- and nationwide he lost to Lincoln in a landslide.

Following the war, McClellan returned to the city to work as chief engineer for the city's Department of Docks, then created his own firm of consulting engineers and accountants. He remained popular: more than a thousand guests attended his daughter May's coming-out party on December 11, 1880. When he died in 1885, his funeral services were held nearby at the Madison Square Presbyterian Church. His son, George McClellan, Jr., went on to serve as mayor of New York from 1904–1909.

087. HORACE GREELEY MONUMENT
Greeley Square, East 32nd Street between Broadway and Sixth Avenue

There are two larger-than-life bronze statues of Horace Greeley in the city. This one honoring the *New York Tribune's* great editor is appropriately located here in Greeley Square. It was dedicated in 1894, two years after the statue downtown near City Hall. The fact that Greeley

Horace Greeley monument.

is the only journalist to be honored by two such memorials is a testament to his stature and influence during the nineteenth century. The Greeley Square statue was created by sculptor Alexander Doyle (1857–1922). Greeley was the first president of the Typographical Union, so the members of the Typographical Society commissioned this work in gratitude for his efforts on their behalf. Oddly enough, Doyle wanted his statue to be placed in City Hall Park—which is where J. Q. A. Ward's sculpture of Greeley eventually ended up. Doyle's work was placed in the square in front of James Gordon Bennett, Jr.'s, new Herald Building on Herald Square, at Broadway and 34th Street. In 1924, long after the deaths of both editors, the *Tribune* merged with the *Herald* to form the *New York Herald Tribune*, which continued publication until 1966.

088. JAMES GORDON BENNETT MEMORIAL
Herald Square, near the intersection of Sixth Avenue and Broadway between West 34th and West 35th Streets

The statue of Minerva, the goddess of wisdom, accompanied by the owls of knowledge and two bell ringers, is dedicated to the memory of James Gordon Bennett (1795–1872), the longtime editor of the *New York Herald*. This sculptural group stood on top of the Herald building, which once faced the park and gave its name to Herald Square. Antonin Jean Paul Carles created the statues in 1894 at a foundry in Paris, then shipped them to New York. When the Herald building was demolished in 1921, the bronzes were placed in storage until 1940, when architect Aymar Embury II arranged the group within this small park.

Bennett was born in Scotland, then emigrated to Canada in 1819 before coming to New York. In 1835, he started the *Herald* as a penny newspaper at a time when other papers were charging as much as a nickel for the news; the *Herald* became extremely popular as a result. As the editor, publisher, and reporter of the *Herald*, Bennett was an innovator. He published the first-ever newspaper interview; shocked readers by featuring the trial of a prostitute on the front page; and was the first to devote space to financial news. During the Civil War, when the newspaper's headquarters were downtown, he put more reporters in the field than anyone else and used illustrations to highlight their stories. The *Herald* was unaligned when it came to politics, but Bennett himself was fiercely anti-Lincoln. Without making editorial statements, he still promoted opposition to Lincoln's policies by frightening his readership with incendiary comments. He wrote that "if Lincoln is elected you will have to compete with the labor of four million emancipated negroes." Bennett backed the Union cause throughout the war but wanted McClellan to replace Lincoln as president in 1864. Even though he was never a supporter of Lincoln or his policies, he was always aware of a good story, and his paper was the first to portray Lincoln as a martyr following the assassination.

In addition to the monument placed here, Bennett Avenue, a street north of West 181st Street near Broadway, is named in Bennett's honor. He maintained a country home in that vicinity.

089. MORGAN LIBRARY
225 Madison Avenue at East 36th Street. Hours: T–Th 10:30 a.m. – 5:00 p.m.; F 10:30 a.m. – 9 p.m.; Sat 10:00 a.m. – 6:00 p.m.; Sun 11:00 a.m. – 6:00 p.m. General information: www.themorgan.org or (212) 685-0008. Admission charge.

J. Pierpont Morgan (1837–1913) was a 24-year-old financier when the Civil War began in 1861. At the time he had a small office on Exchange Place in the financial district. Before long he

James Gordon Bennett Memorial.

became involved in a shady deal involving the sale of defective weapons to the government. Morgan advanced $17,500 to two associates, Simon Stevens and Arthur Eastman, to buy 5,000 obsolete light shoulder rifles from the army. The carbines had already been condemned by the army, but the two sold them back to Gen. John C. Frémont for $110,000 anyway. When Frémont

Morgan Library.

learned the weapons were worthless and probably dangerous, he refused to authorize payment. The War Department investigated and eventually agreed to pay Eastman and Stevens $55,000, but that was not enough to satisfy the crooks, so they sued. The court agreed that the contract was valid and that Morgan should get the full payment for the first 2,500 rifles. This became known as the Hall Carbine Affair.

During the Civil War, Morgan, like all men of age, was required to join the army or provide a substitute, which he did by hiring a replacement for $1,000. With the fortune he amassed during his lifetime, he built the Morgan Library and Museum, one of New York City's treasures.

090. NEW YORK PUBLIC LIBRARY
455 Fifth Avenue and West 42nd Street. Hours and general information: www.nypl.org or (917) 275-6975.

The New York Public Library has one of the greatest research collections of any public library in the world. Thousands of manuscripts, letters, photographs, diaries, books, and other materials pertaining to the Civil War reside here, and all are available to the public. There are important documents by Abraham Lincoln, Horace Greeley, Mathew Brady, Walt Whitman, many Civil War generals (including one of Robert E. Lee's engineering notebooks), the Gideon Welles papers, the General Daniel Sickles papers, and a large number of manuscripts by soldiers from both North and South. One oddity of this vast collection is the complete contents of a Confederate mailbag captured during the war.

New York Public Library.

091. BRYANT PARK and WILLIAM CULLEN BRYANT MEMORIAL
West 42nd Street and Sixth Avenue

For more than 50 years, William Cullen Bryant (1794–1878), for whom Bryant Park is named, served as editor of the *New York Evening Post*, now known as the *New York Post*. Established by Alexander Hamilton in 1801, the *Post* is still in business today, making it the oldest continuously published daily newspaper in America. Now the paper's headquarters are at 1211 Sixth Avenue, a few blocks north of Bryant Park, but during the Civil War its offices were at 53 Liberty Street, in a building near City Hall that no longer exists. In 1829, Bryant bought the *Post* and used the editorial pages to promote free trade and the abolition of slavery. As the war drew near, he became a champion of Abraham Lincoln. As editor in chief, Bryant played a significant role in helping shape and influence New York's political opinions during the Civil War period.

By the time he was 20, William Cullen Bryant had already written his most famous poem, "Thanatopsis," and been hailed a literary prodigy. Later he led the fight to create Central Park. It was Bryant who introduced Abraham Lincoln to the audience at the Cooper Union on February 27, 1860, the evening that Lincoln delivered the speech that propelled him to the presidency. Due to their early friendship, Bryant was able to advise Lincoln on many issues, including cabinet appointments. However, just prior to the beginning of the war, one of the *Post's* editors wrote that "the City of New York belongs almost as much to the South as to the North," expressing the political viewpoint of many of the city's businessmen. Bryant died in his home on West 16th Street on June 12, 1878.

The Croton Reservoir once stood on the site now occupied by Bryant Park. It was demolished in 1884 and the open space thereby created was named in Bryant's honor. In 1911, Herbert Adams (1858–1945) was commissioned to design a memorial to William Cullen Bryant. The great editor is shown seated at the end of the park, looking out from under a canopy designed by the well-known architectural firm of Carrere and Hastings.

William Cullen Bryant Memorial.

092. COLORED ORPHAN ASYLUM
West side of Fifth Avenue between 43rd and 44th Streets

One of the most cowardly acts committed by the draft rioters during the mob's hysterical rampage in July 1863 involved the burning of the Colored Orphan Asylum. The orphanage had been established in 1836 by two white women, Mrs. Anna Shotwell and her niece Mary Murray, at another location and later moved here to property donated by the city. The rioters, intending to wipe out all the black people they could find, set fire to the orphanage. At the time, 237 children under the age of 12 were huddled inside. Only the heroism and quick action of the orphanage staff saved the children from certain death. One precious object, the orphanage Bible, was saved from the fire by an 8-year-old girl as she fled from the flames. A 10-year-old girl was killed when she was hit by falling debris, but the rest survived. In 1867, the asylum was rebuilt at the corner of 143rd Street and Amsterdam Avenue before moving once again to the Riverdale section of the Bronx.

Years ago, several plaques were put up in the city to remind citizens of the horrible actions perpetrated during the draft riots. One plaque marked the spot where William Jones (the first man selected in the draft) lived; a second was on the spot of the draft office itself; and a third was here where the orphanage once stood. All the plaques have since disappeared.

Association for the Benefit of Colored Orphans.

093. HOTEL GERARD
123 West 44th Street, between Sixth Avenue and Broadway

Even the first lady of the Confederacy ended up living in New York City. After Jefferson Davis died in 1889, his widow, Varina Banks Howell Davis (1826–1906), completed the autobiography her husband had begun. That book, published in 1890, did not sell well, and with

123 West 44th Street today.

President Jefferson Davis
and his wife, Varina.

no other means of support Mrs. Davis was forced to move to New York City the following year to become a columnist for Joseph Pulitzer's newspaper, the *New York World*. She and her daughter, Winnie, rented rooms in different residential hotels over the next 15 years. For several of those years they lived in the Hotel Gerard at 123 W. 44th Street, which later became the Hotel Langwell. The elegant building still stands today. Varina Davis offended many Southerners with her move to New York. She compounded her transgression by becoming a friend of Julia Dent Grant, U. S. Grant's widow. At one point she attended a reception where she was introduced to Booker T. Washington, the black head of Tuskegee Institute, another act considered to be socially unacceptable in the South. On October 16, 1906, she died in her room at the Hotel Majestic, which once stood at 115 Central Park West, the site of today's Majestic apartment building. She received a solemn funeral procession through the streets of the city as her body made its way to the train to Richmond, where she was buried beside her husband.

094. NINTH DISTRICT DRAFT OFFICE
Northeast corner of Third Avenue and East 46th Street

Burning of the draft office, July 1863.

Once President Lincoln signed the law calling for a national draft, the next step was to select the draftees. It was agreed that every community would hold a lottery, with names selected at random for conscription into the army. Early on the morning of Saturday, July 11, 1863, a crowd gathered on the pavement outside the draft office on the northeast corner of Third Avenue and 46th Street to listen as the names of 2,000 citizens were selected. (Although the building was number 677 at the time, the numbering system has changed.) At the time, this draft office was on the northern edge of the city, but, due to the nature of the unruly

Selecting names for the draft, 1863.

crowd, the police posted a large force to prevent trouble. When the draft began at 9:00 a.m., the name of William Jones, a resident of 49th Street near Tenth Avenue, was the first selected. Before the day was over, 1,236 names had been drawn and the draft office closed without disturbance, planning to open again on Monday morning. However, the crowd lingered, grew, and began to get out of hand. Many poor Irish immigrants were angry because the law allowed wealthy men to buy their way out of the draft by paying a $300 bounty, an amount well beyond their reach. By the time the draft office opened again on Monday, these citizens were in a rebellious mood, and in no time a full-blown riot erupted. The draft office here was set ablaze, and the fire soon spread to adjoining houses. Since the volunteer firemen were part of the mob, no one put out the fires. For the next few days, the city was at the mercy of the rioters.

095. ST. PATRICK'S CATHEDRAL
Fifth Avenue between East 50th and East 51st Streets. Hours and general information: www.saintpatrickscathedral.org or (212) 753-2261.

Archbishop John Hughes.

The cornerstone for St. Patrick's Cathedral was laid in 1858, but the Civil War interrupted work due to the lack of an adequate labor force. The work resumed after the war, but overall it took 21 years to finish the construction according to the architectural plans of James Renwick, Jr. On May 25, 1879, the church was consecrated and has remained the seat of the Roman Catholic Archdiocese of New York ever since. Archbishop John Hughes, the driving force behind St. Patrick's construction and the city's first archbishop, presided at the groundbreaking but died in 1864 before the building was completed. It was Hughes' idea to build a great cathedral: he hoped it would "be worthy of our increasing numbers, intelligence, and wealth as a religious community, and worthy as a public architectural monument." With this new building, he achieved all those goals. The cathedral was not always so popular: it was originally referred to as "Hughes' Folly" because the site he selected for the church was so far north of the city center at

St. Patrick's Cathedral, New York City.

Postcard view of St. Patrick's Cathedral.

the time; some people believed no one would ever make the trip all the way uptown to worship at St. Patrick's.

It is interesting to note that Archbishop Hughes (whose nickname was "Dagger John" because of the shape of the cross he always used as part of his signature) had been employed as a slave overseer in Maryland shortly after he emigrated from Ireland. Although he supported the Union during the war, he was an opponent of immediate emancipation and frequently made fun of abolitionists. He felt that each state should have the freedom to eliminate slavery at its own pace. In October 1861, President Lincoln invited Archbishop Hughes to the White House to seek his support. Although the Archbishop refused any official appointment, he did agree to visit Europe, where he met with leaders in Paris, Rome, and Dublin to generate support for the Union cause. By the time of his death in 1864, he had become one of the most powerful men in the city

St. Patrick's Cathedral.

and had raised the Catholic church to a position of great respect. He also founded Fordham University, and a statue of the archbishop by Maurice Power can be found at the entrance to the school's main campus in the Bronx. Hughes was originally buried in old St. Patrick's Cathedral downtown, but when the new cathedral was completed his body was exhumed and placed beneath the altar here. You can see the vault door on which his name is inscribed by walking behind the main altar.

Many important ceremonies have taken place at St. Patrick's, including the February 19, 1891, funeral service for Gen. William T. Sherman.

VII. Central Park and the Upper East Side

096. GENERAL WILLIAM TECUMSEH SHERMAN MONUMENT
Grand Army Plaza, Fifth Avenue and West 59th Street

Perhaps only Grant and Lee were more famous during the Civil War than General William Tecumseh Sherman (1820–1891). It was Sherman who led the Union forces on their infamous "March to the Sea" during the autumn of 1864, in the course of which they captured and destroyed Atlanta and cut the Confederacy in half. That campaign helped bring about the end of the long war, but at a terrible price to the country. He was celebrated in the North for his victory but reviled in the South for the "scorched earth" nature of his campaign.

In 1888, Sherman posed for Saint-Gaudens in 18 two-hour sittings for the bust the sculptor used to create the extremely lifelike portrait seen here. Saint-Gaudens combined it with the winged figure of Victory leading Sherman with the palm branch of peace in her hand. The head of Victory was modeled in part on that of the beautiful Elizabeth Cameron, a niece of General Sherman. It took Augustus Saint-Gaudens more than 10 years to create this heroic equestrian group, but when the gilded monument was unveiled on Memorial Day 1903 it was apparent that it

General Sherman monument.

was one of his greatest works. It also happened to be Saint-Gaudens' last major work as a sculptor; he would die just a few years later.

The statue itself rests on a pink granite pedestal designed by architect Charles Follen McKim. Originally the statue was to be placed near Grant's tomb, but both the Grant and Sherman families objected, so this location on 59th Street was selected. It sits at the entrance to Central Park in what is called Grand Army Plaza (not to be confused with Brooklyn's Grand Army Plaza, which is covered later in this book).

General William Tecumseh Sherman.

097. CENTRAL PARK and FREDERICK LAW OLMSTED
Central Park, between Fifth Avenue and Central Park West from West 59th to West 110th Streets. General information: www.centralparknyc.org or (212) 310-6600.

In 1858, architects Frederick Law Olmsted (1822–1903) and Calvert Vaux (1824–1895) won the competition to design Central Park. Olmsted had just published his book *A Journey in the Seaboard Slave States*, one of a series of books in which he condemned slavery, calling it morally odious, expensive, and economically inefficient. Vaux was impressed with Olmsted's egalitarian theories and decided to team up with him, even though Olmstead had never designed anything on the scale of Central Park before. During the Civil War, Olmsted took leave from his duties at the park to become the executive secretary of the U.S. Sanitary Commission, an organization that would eventually become the American Red Cross. He worked tirelessly for the war effort, and even proposed that women be hired to replace men in many jobs so the latter could go off to fight, a radical idea at the time. During the Peninsula Campaign of 1862, Olmsted personally directed the medical teams that treated the sick and wounded in the field.

In November 1861, the North led the largest American amphibious assault—before D-day—against the South Carolina coastal fortifications at Port Royal and Hilton Head Island. Commanding the 1st Brigade in the attack was Gen. Egbert L. Viele, the man who had originally held the position of engineer in chief of Central Park from 1856 to 1858. Although work on the park continued sporadically throughout the war, men were continually drawn away to fight. During the Draft Riots of 1863, most of the immigrant work force left their jobs here to take part in the rioting and looting. The park was not officially completed until 1873.

Central Park in Winter from *Harper's Weekly*.

098. CENTRAL PARK ARMORY, ALSO CALLED "THE ARSENAL"
830 Fifth Avenue, in Central Park at 64th Street. Open during business hours.

When the Draft Riots erupted on Monday, July 13, 1863, many believed there were no military forces at all in the city, and therefore the mobs ran rampant. But in actuality two cavalry troops and one regiment of the New York National Guard were on hand at the time. The cavalry was in the city as an honor guard for the funeral of Brig. Gen. Samuel K. Zook (1821–1863), who had been killed in action at Gettysburg on July 3. These forces were under the command of Maj. Gen. Charles W. Sandford (1796–1878). When the violence started, Sandford split his forces into three groups and sent one section to each of the three major arsenals to guard against looting. Soldiers were sent here to the Central Park Armory, the main storehouse for the munitions of the state of New York. In addition to being a munitions dump, the 1848 building was also being used as the headquarters for the 11th Police Precinct. Due to the presence of the heavily armed soldiers, the mob never attacked this location, instead focusing its attention on easier targets. Note the carved doorway depicting an eagle on a pile of cannon balls, typical of arsenal ornamentation at the time.

The Arsenal.

099. WILLIAM SHAKESPEARE MEMORIAL
The Mall in Central Park, near East 66th Street

On April 23, 1864, the foundation stone for a statue of William Shakespeare was laid at the southern end of the Mall, but it wasn't until 1870 that the bronze figure by sculptor John Quincy Adams Ward was unveiled. It stands on a molded granite base designed by Jacob Wrey Mould and was funded by donations from New York citizens and the Shakespeare Tricentennial Committee. What is not as well known is that a good deal of the money for the sculpture came from a fundraising performance of *Julius Caesar* in which three actor brothers, Edwin, Junius, and John Wilkes Booth, performed together—for the first and only time—at the Winter Garden Theatre on November 25, 1864. They raised the princely sum of $3,500, which they contributed toward the creation of this statue of the world's greatest playwright.

William Shakespeare Memorial.

100. SEVENTH REGIMENT MEMORIAL
Central Park, West Drive near West 68th Street

"The Lone Sentry," the memorial sculpture by John Quincy Adams Ward that honors the soldiers of New York's 7th Regiment, stands guard over West Drive in Central Park. The bronze statue was created in 1869 and placed on a pedestal designed by Richard Morris Hunt in 1874. Ward's sculpture served as the model for countless Civil War monuments erected on village greens across America in the years after the war. In fact, so many were produced that they appeared for sale in catalogues and could be ordered by mail.

In this case, the monument honors the 58 men of the 7th Regiment who lost their lives in service of the Union. They were among the first New Yorkers to enlist after President Lincoln called for volunteers in April 1861. The motto of the regiment, "Pro Patria Et Gloria," is engraved on all four sides of the base along with a shield of stars and stripes.

Seventh Regiment Memorial.

101. GENERAL ULYSSES S. GRANT RESIDENCE
3 East 66th Street

In 1879, supporters gave General and Mrs. Ulysses S. Grant an elegant brownstone house befitting a former president of the United States. It once stood at this site, but the home was demolished in 1928 to make way for the apartment building standing there now. A plaque affixed to the current building notes the earlier residence of one of America's most beloved citizens. It was supporters who bought the house for Grant because he had fallen on hard times, a victim of corrupt friends and poor business decisions, yet the people still loved him and wanted to show their appreciation for all he had done to preserve the Union. In 1884, the general's company,

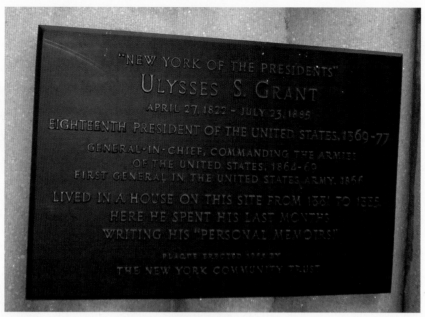

Historical marker for Grant's home.

Grant & Ward, went bankrupt, leaving him penniless, and one of his creditors, William Vanderbilt, took over the house. However, Vanderbilt was also a close and generous friend of Grant, so he arranged for the Grants to remain in their house as long as they wanted, rent free.

It was in this house that the general's last courageous act played out. The same year as his final bankruptcy, Grant was diagnosed with terminal cancer of the mouth. Knowing that he would soon die, he worked tirelessly, ignoring great pain, to complete his memoirs, hoping to replace some of the money he had lost in business. It became a race against time, but somehow he managed to finish his book on July 19, 1885, just four days before his death. Although Grant was at his summer retreat when death finally came, he wrote most of the book in his home here. When published, the book became a tremendously popular bestseller, providing more than enough profits to support his family.

102. PARK AVENUE ARMORY, or NEW 7th REGIMENT ARMORY
643 Park Avenue, between East 66th and 67th Streets. Hours and general information: www.armoryonpark.org or (212) 744-8180.

The beautiful current building did not exist during the Civil War; it was constructed between 1878 and 1880. It replaced the 7th Regiment Armory that had been in service downtown on Third Avenue at 7th Street during the war. The new building was designed by an architect who was a veteran of the regiment, Charles W. Clinton. This location has an exceptional collection of memorabilia, flags, and weapons that moved here with the regiment. The armory was the home of the "Silk Stocking" regiment, and, true to its name, when this building was dedicated in 1880, the members of the regiment marched to their new quarters to host a grand ball for members of New York's high society.

Park Avenue Armory.

103. STEPHEN VINCENT BENÉT'S RESIDENCE
215 East 68th Street

The last home of author Stephen Vincent Benét (1898–1943) once stood on this block, now replaced by high-rise apartment buildings. He is perhaps best known for his book-length poem on a Civil War theme entitled *John Brown's Body*. That book won him the Pulitzer Prize in 1929 and propelled him on to a great literary career that included winning the O. Henry Award for his story *The Devil and Daniel Webster* in 1937. Benét purchased this house in 1939 and died here on March 13, 1943, after suffering a heart attack at 44. *John Brown's Body* was later presented as a play on Broadway in 1953 starring Raymond Massey, Judith Anderson, and Tyrone Power under the direction of Charles Laughton. Massey, who went on to play John

Stephen Vincent Benét.

Brown again in the 1955 movie *Seven Angry Men*, is also famous for his portrayal of Abraham Lincoln in the play and film version of *Abe Lincoln in Illinois*.

104. METROPOLITAN MUSEUM OF ART
1000 Fifth Avenue, in Central Park at East 82nd Street. Hours: T–Th 9:30 a.m. – 5:30 p.m.; F–Sat 9:30 a.m. – 9:00 p.m.; Sun 9:30 a.m. – 5:30 p.m. General information: www.metmuseum.org or (212) 535-7710. Admission charge.

Edouard Manet's painting "The *Kearsarge* at Boulogne."

Many visitors might not realize that the collections within the Metropolitan Museum of Art display some wonderful items related to the Civil War period. One of these masterpieces is an 1864 painting by Edouard Manet entitled "The *Kearsarge* at Boulogne." In June of 1864, an important naval engagement of the American war took place off the coast of France. The USS

Metropolitan Museum of Art.

Kearsarge attacked and destroyed the CSS *Alabama*, a Confederate raider that had been harassing the North's shipping and the Union blockade of Southern ports. French spectators crowded the shoreline to watch the sinking of the *Alabama*, and artist Manet rushed to the port of Boulogne. While he did not arrive in time to witness the battle, he did see the *Kearsarge* in dock and afterwards painted a picture of the clash.

Also in the museum are many well-known pieces, including Winslow Homer's "Prisoners at the Front" and "Veteran in a New Field"; Thomas Hovenden's "The Last Moments of John Brown"; Daniel Chester French's statue "Mourning Visit"; and portraits of many Civil War dignitaries. The American Paintings collection also contains the interesting "A Bit of War History" canvas by Thomas Waterman Wood. This triptych traces the evolution of an African-American from free man to recruit to wounded veteran. The Costume Institute contains uniforms and period clothing and the Musical Instruments section displays regimental drums and various wind instruments. The American wing includes furniture and decorative articles from the period, including an armchair made by Herter Brothers identical to the ones used by Grant in the White House. Lesser known works include William W. Story's sculpture "The Libyan Sibyl," an allegory of the sin of slavery, and Charles Elliott's portrait of Mathew Brady. These are only a few examples of the treasures displayed in the museum's galleries.

105. CARL SCHURZ PARK and GRACIE MANSION
East End Avenue, from East 84th to East 90th Streets. Hours: W 10:00 a.m. – 2:00 p.m. General information: www.nyc.gov/html/om/html/gracie.html.

This park was named in honor of Carl Schurz (1829–1906), who became well known in New York for his work as a newspaper editor and civic reformer. More about his life and involvement with the Civil War can be found in the description of his memorial (site 114) that overlooks

Gracie Mansion, ca. 1875.

Gracie Mansion.

Morningside Park near Columbia University. Schurz's home was at 24 East 91st Street but is no longer standing.

Gracie Mansion was built in 1799 as the country home of the wealthy Scottish-born merchant and shipping magnate Archibald Gracie (1755–1829). When Gracie first arrived in America, he established a mercantile company in New York, but later moved to Virginia to become involved in the exportation of tobacco. By 1798, when he purchased the land that Gracie Mansion would be built upon, he was very well off. His son Archibald II moved to Mobile, Alabama, to oversee the production of the cotton that his father was shipping to Europe. As a result, his son Archibald III was born in Mobile; the latter went into the banking end of his family's cotton business there. At the outbreak of the Civil War, Archibald Gracie III enlisted in the Southern army and, due to his valiant service in the campaign at Huntsville, Tennessee, in 1862, was promoted to the rank of brigadier general. His regiment played a leading role in the battle of Chickamauga, during which it lost over 700 men. Later at Petersburg, General Gracie himself was credited with saving Gen. Robert E. Lee's life. Still later in the series of battles around Petersburg, Gracie was severely wounded by an exploding artillery shell and died on December 2, 1864, the day after his 32nd birthday. He was interred in the Bronx in the Woodlawn Cemetery. Today Gracie Mansion is the official residence of New York City's mayors.

106. MUSEUM OF THE CITY OF NEW YORK
1220 Fifth Avenue, at 103rd Street. Hours: T–Sun 10:00 a.m. – 5:00 p.m. General information: www.mcny.org or (212) 534-1672. Admission charge.

The museum here has one of the finest collections of Civil War memorabilia in the city. It often mounts exhibitions that display items of Civil War interest. Within the collection are paintings, uniforms, furniture, weapons, prints, posters, and photographs from the era as well as Harry Peters' collection of Currier and Ives prints.

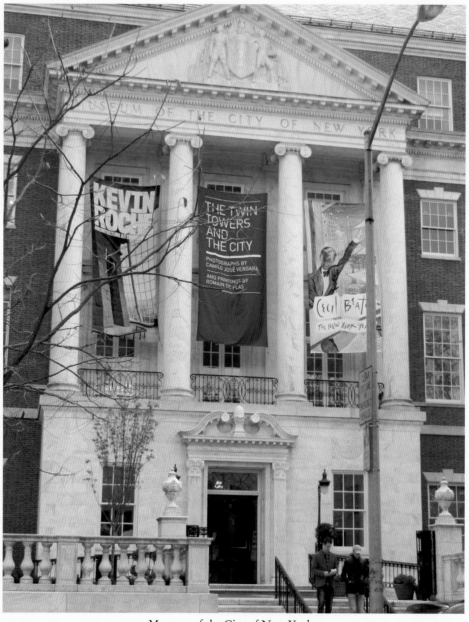

Museum of the City of New York.

VIII. The Upper West Side, Harlem, and Washington Heights

107. GENERAL FITZ JOHN PORTER RESIDENCE
68 West 68th Street

After retiring from the military, Gen. Fitz John Porter (1822–1901) lived in the house still standing at 68 West 68th Street. During those years Porter was active in New York City government and served as police commissioner, commissioner of public works, and fire commissioner before his death in 1901. In August 1862, at the second battle of Bull Run, General Porter was ordered to attack a superior force led by Generals Jackson and Longstreet. But Porter felt the strategy would be suicide, so he delayed engagement until the following day—at which time his corps of 5,000 men was totally destroyed by 30,000 Confederates, just as he had predicted. After the battle, he was court-martialed for disobedience and failure to act under orders. Many of his supporters claimed that the court-martial was politically motivated, since Porter was a close friend of and strong advocate for General McClellan, who at the time was about to be relieved of

General Porter's house.

duty by President Lincoln. For more than 20 years Porter fought to clear his name, and in 1886 President Arthur overturned his court-martial and his commission was restored. General Porter was buried with honors in Brooklyn's Green-Wood Cemetery.

108. GENERAL SHERMAN RESIDENCE
75 West 71st Street

General William Tecumseh Sherman.

During the last few years of his life, Gen. William Tecumseh Sherman lived in a house at 75 West 71st Street which is no longer standing. Here General Sherman died on February 14, 1891, at the age of 71. This block was entirely draped in black and all the flags in the city flew at half-staff in his honor. The newspapers of the day noted that it was a pageant worthy of General Sherman. Tens of thousands of people crowded the neighborhood and lined the streets through which his flag-covered casket was drawn by five coal-black horses. Presidents Grover Cleveland and Rutherford B. Hayes came to the house to pay their last respects, as did a host of generals including Butterfield, Schofield, Howard, Slocum, Sickles, Dodge, Corse, Swayne, Woodford, Wright, and Moore, and Admirals Braine and Green. Even his old opponent Confederate Gen. Joseph E. Johnston turned out to mourn with the others. The procession took nearly two and a half hours to pass. Bringing up the rear, a soldier led a black horse with the general's saddle on its back, his now-empty boots reversed, as tradition dictates.

General Sherman is honored in several other ways in the neighborhood. Tiny Sherman Square, at the intersection of Broadway, Amsterdam Avenue, and West 70th Street, was dedicated shortly after the general's death in 1891. His name is also remembered in nearby Tecumseh Playground at the corner of Amsterdam Avenue and West 77th Street.

109. NEW YORK HISTORICAL SOCIETY
170 Central Park West, at West 77th Street. Hours: T–Th, Sat 10:00 a.m. – 6:00 p.m., F 10:00 a.m. – 8:00 p.m., Sun 11:00 a.m. – 5:45 p.m. General information: www.nyhistory.org or (212) 873-3400. Admission charge.

The New York Historical Society has been a repository for the history of New York City for more than 200 years, and it is rich in materials that deal with the Civil War. Perhaps no other museum in the city has documented that period as well as the Historical Society. Recently a

New York Historical Society.

bronze statue of Abraham Lincoln was placed on the front steps of the museum. The society's collections contain thousands of photographs, paintings, prints, letters, diaries, posters, uniforms (including one made of "shoddy" by Brooks Brothers), weapons, money, stamps, and other items. One item of particular interest is the actual lottery wheel used to select the names of Civil War draftees. That process led directly to the infamous Draft Riots of 1863. The museum also owns a fragment of the Union flag that flew over Fort Sumter in 1861, Daniel Chester French's portrait busts of Abraham Lincoln and General Sherman, a 25-foot-long petition from the citizens of New York requesting that President Lincoln authorize the creation of black regiments, the half-model used in the construction of the USS *Monitor*, Eastman Johnson's depiction of "Negro Life in the South, 1859," and Louis Lang's monumental history painting of the "Return of the 69th (Irish) Regiment from the Seat of War, 1862." Even General Grant's handwritten terms of surrender that he delivered to General Lee at Appomattox are part of these extensive collections.

110. SOLDIERS' AND SAILORS' MEMORIAL
Riverside Drive at West 89th Street

Manhattan's Soldiers' and Sailors' Memorial was unveiled on Memorial Day 1902, the work of architects Charles (1860–1944) and Arthur Stoughton (1867–1955). It consists of a particularly beautiful 96-foot-tall, circular, white-marble temple that is ringed by a colonnade of a dozen Corinthian columns and guarded by two cannon. Originally this "Temple of Fame" in honor of the Civil War dead was to be located in Grand Army Plaza on Fifth Avenue at 59th Street, where the Pulitzer Fountain stands today, but city officials later selected this spot instead. Around the top of the monument are carved the words, "To The Memory Of The Brave Soldiers And Sailors Who Saved The Union." The memorial also displays the names of Farragut, Sherman, Porter, and others, along with the names of battles in which New York regiments saw action.

Soldiers' and Sailors' Memorial.

111. THOMAS DIXON RESIDENCE
61 West 94th Street

During his long life, Thomas F. Dixon, Jr. (1864–1946), did a little bit of everything. He was a Baptist minister, playwright, lecturer, state legislator, lawyer, and author. It is as an author that he is of interest to students of Civil War history, for he is the man who wrote *The Clansman*, the book that in 1915 was turned into D. W. Griffith's film *The Birth of a Nation*. That movie became

59 West 94th Street.

the highest grossing film of the silent era, but it remains controversial a hundred years later because of its racist portrayal of African-Americans. The film is also credited with reviving the long-dormant Ku Klux Klan that same year. In *The Clansman*, Dixon opined that Reconstruction was a total disaster and that blacks could never be integrated into Southern society. After moving to New York in 1889 to practice as a Baptist minister, Dixon became disillusioned with his denomination and began to preach at a nondenominational church on 23rd Street. He continued as pastor there until 1899, living in a house that stood at 61 West 94th Street. Although that house is no longer there, the one next door at number 59 West 94th is very much like Dixon's home. Reverend Dixon retired from the ministry to devote himself full-time to writing. He published his first book, *The Leopard's Spots*, in 1902, and then *The Clansman* in 1905. Both illustrated his contempt for black people.

Thomas Dixon.

112. GENERAL FRANZ SIGEL MONUMENT
Riverside Drive and West 106th Street

The bronze monument to Franz Sigel (1824–1902) by sculptor Karl Bitter (1867–1915) is one of the latter's most beautiful equestrian statues in the city. It was dedicated in 1907. The horse and rider stand overlooking the Hudson River, on a pedestal designed by Willis Bosworth. General Siegel was a German-born American who encouraged many immigrants in his ethnic community to enlist. His regiment helped keep Missouri and the important federal arsenal located there in Union hands. Throughout the war, Sigel held several commissions and commanded troops during the battles of Carthage, Pea Ridge, Wilson's Creek, and Second Bull Run, and in the Valley campaigns of 1864. When the general died in 1902, his body was buried in Woodlawn Cemetery. A park was named after him along the Grand Concourse in the Bronx between East 151st and 158th Streets, not far from the home on Mott Avenue (now the Grand Concourse) where he lived during the latter part of his life.

General Franz Sigel monument.

113. FREDERICK DOUGLASS CIRCLE
Central Park West at West 110th Street

The intersection where Central Park West becomes Eighth Avenue at 110th Street has been known since 1950 as Frederick Douglass Circle. The designation honors Douglass, who was born a slave in the South in 1818 and was given the name Frederick Augustus Washington Bailey by his owners. As an adult he escaped from slavery to become a crusading abolitionist, author, and orator of renown. Douglass changed his name after he fled Maryland and came to New York, arriving at the safe house of David Ruggles on September 4, 1838. The ex-slave believed that abolition should be achieved by peaceful methods, so he declined John Brown's offer to take part in the armed raid on Harper's Ferry. At the time of the Civil War, Douglass was perhaps the most famous black man in America. During the war, he argued in favor of the use of black soldiers, saying that people should be allowed to fight for their own freedom. During the 1864 presidential election, Douglass supported John C. Frémont after becoming disenchanted with Abraham

Frederick Douglas Memorial.

Lincoln. He felt Lincoln had dragged his feet on emancipation and did not go far enough, since he did not grant black freedmen the right to vote. Douglass also supported the Union cause by acting as a recruiter for Massachusetts' 54th Regiment. In 1882, his autobiography, *Life and Times of Frederick Douglass*, was published and has been in print ever since. Douglass passed away in 1895.

In 2011, the city officially dedicated the Frederick Douglass Memorial. The eight-foot-tall bronze sculpture was created by Hungarian artist Gabriel Koren. The plaza includes a fountain, paving, and other markers designed by the Harlem-based artist Algernon Miller. The representation of the Big Dipper constellation evokes the stars that escaping slaves used to navigate their way north via the Underground Railroad.

114. GENERAL CARL SCHURZ MONUMENT
Morningside Drive at West 116th Street

Although Carl Schurz is better known as a statesman and reformer, the German-American immigrant also served as a general in the Union army during the Civil War. As a politician he backed William H. Seward against Lincoln for the Republican nomination in 1860. However, after Seward's defeat, Schurz was appointed to the committee delegated to inform Lincoln he had won his party's nomination, and Lincoln made Schurz ambassador to Spain in 1861. Later that same year, Schurz asked for a military commission. As a brigadier general he commanded troops at the second battle of Bull Run, then was promoted to major general before fighting at the battle of Chancellorsville. He saw action at Gettysburg and Chattanooga and with Sherman in North Carolina near the end of the war. In 1881, Schurz moved to New

(Top right) General Carl Schurz Monument;
(Above) General Carl Schurz Monument (detail).

York City, where he worked for various newspapers and conducted private business ventures until his death in 1906.

This statue was cast in bronze by sculptor Karl Bitter and placed on a granite exedra made by Henry Bacon, the designer of the Lincoln Memorial in Washington, DC. The full-length portrait was an important commission for Bitter and he executed it perfectly, uniting the figure within the architectural framework. It was Bitter who selected the dramatic site as well, and in 1913 the monument was unveiled on this bluff overlooking Morningside Park. The inscription reads: "Carl Schurz, a Defender of Liberty, and a Friend of Human Rights." The reliefs on the panels illustrate Schurz' philosophy, showing his desire to defend liberty, to destroy the chains of slavery, and to make peace with Native Americans.

115. GENERAL GRANT NATIONAL MEMORIAL, ALSO CALLED GRANT'S TOMB
Riverside Drive at West 122nd Street. Hours: Daily 9:00 a.m. – 5:00 p.m. General information: www.nps.gov/gegr or (212) 666-1640.

Perhaps the most famous Civil War monument in the city is Grant's Tomb. It was dedicated in 1897 with architect John Duncan (1855–1929) and sculptor John Massey Rhind (1860–1936) in attendance. Standing 150 feet tall, this is the largest tomb in America. The mausoleum commands a sweeping view of the Hudson River and the New Jersey Palisades. When General Grant died in 1885, he was reputed to be the most popular man in America. Nearly 90,000 people raised $600,000 for this monument, and one million people turned out to witness its dedication by President McKinley on Grant's birthday, April 27, 1897. It remained the city's number one tourist attraction until after the First World War.

General Grant himself needs no introduction. He led the Northern forces to their final victories of the Civil War. He fought in numerous battles and distinguished himself as a great military commander. After the war, he was elected the 18th president of the United States. His post-military career was marred by the corruption of his associates, bankruptcy, and disappointment. Through a heroic effort, he was able to complete his autobiography only a few days before his death, and that publication restored his family's fortune.

The memorial is a classic structure that resembles an Ionic temple with a conical roof. Inscribed above the door are Grant's famous words "Let Us Have Peace." Grant lies entombed next to his wife Julia Dent Grant, and inside the rotunda viewers can look down on the two

Grant's Tomb today.

sarcophagi or walk down a flight of stairs for a closer look. In death he is surrounded by busts of his favorite generals: Sherman, Sheridan, Thomas, McPherson, and Ord. In each corner of the building there are battle flags and other displays of Civil War memorabilia, as well as a gift shop.

North of Grant's tomb is a grove of ginkgo trees planted in Grant's honor by Li Hongzhang, the greatest Chinese statesman of the nineteenth century. A flagstaff outside the mausoleum honors Brig. Gen. Horace Porter, Grant's aide-de-camp, and a bronze plaque reminds us of his contributions to the country. Porter was also the president of the Grant Monument Association and helped raise the $600,000 needed to construct the tomb.

116. GENERAL DANIEL BUTTERFIELD STATUE
Sakura Park, Claremont Avenue and West 122nd Street

Across the street from Grant's Tomb is a small park containing a statue of Union general Daniel Butterfield (1831–1901). The sculptor was the distinguished artist John Gutzon de la Mothe Borglum (1867–1941), known to most schoolchildren as the man who created Mount Rushmore. In 1917, 10 years before he began work on the colossal heads of Washington, Jefferson, Roosevelt, and Lincoln in South Dakota, he created this statue to honor the man who wrote the melancholy bugle tune "Taps." Although Butterfield enjoyed a long career during which he rose to the rank of major general and the position of chief of staff of the Army of the Potomac, he is best known for his musical composition. After the war, he became a successful businessman, living at 37 West 12th Street in a house now replaced by the Butterfield House apartments. His wife left money in her will to erect this statue. It depicts General Butterfield standing on top of Little Round Top during the battle of Gettysburg, during which he served as General Meade's chief of staff and was wounded on the third day. Interestingly, when the statue was completed the executors of her will did not believe it was an accurate likeness of Butterfield, so refused to make the final payments.

Statue of General Daniel Butterfield.

117. GENERAL WINFIELD SCOTT HANCOCK STATUE
Hancock Square, at the intersection of Manhattan Avenue, St. Nicholas Avenue, and West 124th Street

One of the Union's most successful generals of the Civil War was Winfield Scott Hancock (1824–1886). He is honored in this square with a statue by James Wilson Alexander MacDonald (1824–1908). It is a larger-than-life bronze bust of the general mounted on a granite pedestal. Although not as well known today, Hancock was extremely famous in his day, and came close to being elected president in 1880; he lost to James Garfield by only a slim margin. Many believe it was his leadership that resulted in Union victory at Gettysburg. He commanded troops of the Army of the Potomac bravely in many other battles, including the Peninsula Campaign, Antietam, Fredericksburg, Chancellorsville, the Wilderness, Spotsylvania, and Cold Harbor. After the war, Hancock was appointed to supervise the execution of the Booth conspirators who were convicted in their plot to assassinate Lincoln. In 1890, this monument was commissioned by the members of Hancock Post 259, Grand Army of the Republic, in honor of their commander, and it was unveiled three years later.

Statue of General Hancock.

118. ABRAHAM LINCOLN AND CHILD STATUE
Madison Avenue near East 133rd Street

As a young student, sculptor Charles Keck (1875–1951) apprenticed with the great American artist Augustus Saint-Gaudens. This bronze pair of larger-than-life figures sits on a granite base and shows Abraham Lincoln with a young boy, symbolizing his role as a man of the people and a friend to children. The memorial was unveiled in 1948, near the end of the New York artist's long life. It is appropriately located amidst the large complex of public apartments known as the Lincoln Houses. Keck's rendering of the Great Seal of the Commonwealth of Virginia appears on that state's flag.

Abraham Lincoln and Child.

119. SCHOMBURG CENTER FOR RESEARCH IN BLACK CULTURE
515 Malcolm X Boulevard, at West 135th Street.
Hours: T–Th 12:00 p.m. – 8:00 p.m., F–Sat 10:00 a.m. – 6:00 p.m.
General information: www.nypl.org/locations/schomburg or (212) 491-2200.

This special branch of the New York Public Library houses one of the greatest collections relating to African-American history in the country. The center's collections contain a large number of artifacts and documents relating to slavery in America, including original slave shackles, identification tags, and slaveship cargo lists. The new building was erected in 1978 and features a gallery that often displays articles of Civil War interest.

Schomburg Library.

120. GENERAL ALEXANDER STEWART WEBB STATUE
City College Campus, West 139th Street and Convent Avenue

The monument to Gen. Alexander Stewart Webb (1835–1911) is located on the City College campus. This is a fitting place for that tribute, since Webb became president of the college in 1869 and served in that capacity until 1902. As a major general during the war, he commanded the

Philadelphia Brigade in the battles of Chancellorsville and Gettysburg. Upon his death in 1911, college alumni raised the money for this remembrance. They called on sculptor John Massey Rhind to execute the larger-than-life statue, which was unveiled in 1917. The sword Webb holds in his hand was vandalized long ago but has now been restored. There is a duplicate of this statue on the battlefield at Gettysburg where Webb won the Congressional Medal of Honor for repulsing Pickett's Charge.

Statue of General Alexander Stewart Webb.

121. ABRAHAM LINCOLN BUST
City College Campus, Shepard Hall at West 139th Street and Convent Avenue

This three-foot-tall bust of Abraham Lincoln is by the famed sculptor of Mount Rushmore, Gutzon Borglum. It was cast in bronze in 1928 and placed here, a gift to the college from the class of 1910. From 1927 to 1941, Borglum was busy with the 60-foot-tall Mt. Rushmore project; this statue is one of many he created of Lincoln during the course of that work. So much did the sculptor admire the 16th President that he named his son Lincoln Borglum. Once engraved on the base were Lincoln's immortal words, "With Malice Toward None, With Charity For All," but that stone pedestal was replaced with a more modest wooden one.

Early picture of Lincoln bust in Borglum's studio.

122. TRINITY CEMETERY
West 155th Street, between Broadway and Amsterdam Avenue. Hours: Daily 9:00 a.m. – 4:00 p.m. General information: www.trinitywallstreet.org or (212) 368-1600.

Fernando Wood, the first of New York's three Civil War mayors, is buried in the eastern division of this cemetery. His grave is marked by a tall stele capped with a traditional Victorian symbol of mourning, the draped urn. Although not born rich, by the time of his death in 1881, Wood had become a very wealthy man due to his investments in shipping and real estate. He believed that business interests in New York would suffer as a result of the loss of Southern trade if war was declared, so at the beginning of the war he proposed that the city secede from the Union to become a free city, allied with neither North nor South. His fears proved to be unfounded, because the profits made from the business of war more than made up for the loss of the cotton trade. Wood was elected mayor in 1854, lost his bid for re-election, but was elected once more in 1860. In politics he was a Democrat, sympathetic toward the Southern cause—and it may come as a surprise to learn that a large percentage of New Yorkers agreed with him. These Northerners

Grave of Mayor Fernando Wood.

with Southern leanings were nicknamed "Copperheads" after the poisonous snake. Wood was so discouraged by Abraham Lincoln's election that he refused to fly the American flag over City Hall on the day of Lincoln's inauguration.

In 1862, Wood was elected to the House of Representatives, and the following year joined with New York's Governor Horatio Seymour to found the Society for the Diffusion of Political Knowledge. They published pamphlets attacking the continuation of the war and opposing emancipation of the slaves. In June 1863, they rented Cooper Union's Great Hall for a multi-event Peace Convention that was attended by more than 30,000 people. A controversial subject at the convention concerned the abolition of slavery. Many feared that the city would be overrun by free blacks, willing to work for a fraction of what white workers had been earning. Fernando Wood, the owner of the *Daily News* and brother of its editor, Benjamin, published articles in the newspaper on July 13 of that year that suggested as much. All this helped fan the flames of the Draft Riots that erupted the same day. At this time Mayor Wood lived at 122 Second Avenue, but spent a good deal of time at his "country" residence, called Wood Lawn, near the present-day intersection of Broadway and West 77th Street.

123. WADSWORTH AVENUE
North of West 172nd Street, between Broadway and St. Nicholas Avenue

General James Wadsworth.

This New York street was named in honor of Brig. Gen. James Samuel Wadsworth (1807–1864). He was born in 1807 in Geneseo, a town far from New York City in the western part of New York State. Wadsworth was a wealthy Republican landowner and philanthropist before the war who distinguished himself in battle with the Union army. Although he had no prior military background, he was appointed a major general in May 1861 and served as aide-de-camp to General McDowell during the first battle of Bull Run. While serving in the army he ran for governor of the state in 1862 but was defeated by the Democrat Horatio Seymour. Fifty-four years old at the start of the war, he laudably sacrificed his comfortable life to defend the Union. During the battle of Gettysburg his division held off Confederate forces for three days, suffering heavy losses in the process. Wadsworth was killed during the battle of the Wilderness in 1864, after having two horses shot out from under him.

The Bronx

124. FORT SCHUYLER
6 Pennyfield Avenue, Throgs Neck, The Bronx. Hours: M–Sat 9:00 a.m. – 4:00 p.m. General information: www.sunymaritime.edu/Maritime%20Museum or (718) 409-7218.

Fort Schuyler was built to defend the northern water approach to New York City via Long Island Sound. Although begun in 1833, the fort was not quite finished when it was dedicated in 1856. Fort Schuyler faces Fort Totten on the Queens side of the river, completing a perfect cross-fire defense. During the Civil War, these forts were used as prisons to detain Confederate soldiers. Nearly 500 prisoners were held here, including deserters from the Union army and other

Fort Schuyler as seen from Fort Totten.

miscreants. Unlike other, more notorious prisons, Fort Schuyler was considered to be clean and well run; in fact, no one died of disease here during the war, a remarkable statistic. Fresh recruits with Duryea's Zouaves and the Irish Brigade who were heading off to battle were equipped and trained at this fort as well.

Also attached to Fort Schuyler was a hospital complex capable of accommodating 2,500 patients. The 132 mostly male nurses treated both Union casualties and Confederate prisoners. Following the battle at Gettysburg, nearly a thousand wounded men were sent to this hospital for treatment. In 1934, the fort was decommissioned. It is now part of the State University of New York Maritime College, a component of the SUNY system. A section of the building serves as a museum whose displays document the history of the fort.

125. HALL OF FAME FOR GREAT AMERICANS
Bronx Community College, 2183 University Avenue and West 181st Street, The Bronx. Hours: Daily 10:00 a.m. – 5:00 p.m. General information: www.bcc.cuny.edu/halloffame or (718) 289-5161.

A forgotten institution of bygone New York still exists at the Bronx Community College, now part of the CUNY system. Here you will find the original Hall of Fame for Great Americans, which was established in 1900 as the focal point of the New York University campus then at this location. It is a semicircular colonnade that curves for over 200 yards and was originally meant to encompass the Gould Memorial Library. The memorial was designed by the architectural firm of McKim, Mead and White to house busts of notable Americans who by thought and deed had served mankind. A bronze panel designed by Tiffany Studios is affixed to the base of each bust giving detailed information about the honoree. The 97 figures around the imposing colonnade include such Civil War-era luminaries as Lincoln, Grant, Lee, Farragut, Sherman, Stonewall Jackson, Walt Whitman, William Cullen Bryant, Henry Ward Beecher, Edwin Booth, and Harriet Beecher Stowe. Jefferson Davis was nominated twice but not elected.

126. THE BRONX COUNTY HISTORICAL SOCIETY
3309 Bainbridge Avenue, The Bronx. Hours: T–Th 9:00 a.m. – 5:00 p.m. General information: www.bronxhistoricalsociety.org or (718) 881-8900.

The Bronx County Historical Society and Library often display items that relate to the history of this borough. Within their collection are examples of Civil War diaries, a Union cavalry saber with scabbard, Union soldiers' discharge documents, photographs, and scrapbooks that focus on the role of the Bronx during the war. Near their headquarters is a monument entitled the "Bronx River Soldier." Sculpted in granite by John Grignola (1861–1912), the piece was intended to adorn a grave in the nearby Woodlawn Cemetery but was never used. Later it was placed on a granite pier in the Bronx River. In 1964, the sculpture fell into the river but was salvaged and installed here.

The Hall of Fame today.

Bronx River Soldier.

127. WOODLAWN CEMETERY and VAN CORTLANDT PARK
Webster Avenue and East 233rd Street, The Bronx. Hours: Daily
8:30 a.m. – 5:00 p.m. General information: www.thewoodlawncemetery.org or
(718) 920-0500.

Woodlawn is one of largest cemeteries in New York City: it has received more than 300,000 burials. It was opened in 1863, midway through the Civil War, and is the final resting place of many veterans from both North and South. As one of the nation's most renowned cemeteries, Woodlawn contains the graves of a legion of dignitaries. Admiral David G. Farragut, whose beautiful public memorial is located in Madison Square, was interred in Woodlawn in 1870. His

General Franz Sigel's grave.

headstone features traditional nautical symbols: a broken mast with rope, belaying pins, a sextant, and hilts of swords. Near Farragut is another U.S. naval officer, Commodore Henry Eagle. It was Eagle who fired the first offensive shot from a vessel during the Civil War at Newell's Point, Virginia.

Admiral David Farragut's grave.

Among the soldiers buried in Woodlawn are Gen. Franz Sigel, whose equestrian statue on the Upper West Side guards Riverside Drive; Col. Benjamin Bristow, who captured the Confederate raider Gen. John Hunt Morgan; and Gen. Richard Busteed, who served in the Yorktown campaign. The Confederacy is also well represented in the cemetery. Here is found the grave of

General Tilghman's grave.

Gen. Lloyd Tilghman, who fought against Grant on the Tennessee River. Although Tilghman was originally buried in the South following his death in 1863 at the battle of Champion Hill, his family brought his remains north to the family plot in 1901. The Southern Gen. Archibald Gracie III is also buried here, although his headstone is badly weathered and difficult to identify. He was a member of the family that built Gracie Mansion, now the official home of New York's mayors. Confederate Brig. Gen. Zachariah C. Deas served as aide-de-camp to Gen. Joseph E. Johnston at the first battle of Bull Run, fought bravely for the South at Shiloh and Chickamauga, and was wounded in battle several times. After his death he was buried in Woodlawn.

Civil War noncombatants figure in Woodlawn's roster, too. Mary "Mamie" Lincoln Isham, the president's granddaughter, and Cornelius H. Delamater, whose iron works produced the hardware for the USS *Monitor*, are buried here, as is Frank Leslie, the publisher of *Frank Leslie's Illustrated Weekly*. That newspaper's illustrations from the battlefield helped inform the public about the grim realities of war. Illustrator Thomas Nast, who began his career making political cartoons about the Civil War and Reconstruction, lies nearby. Due to the popularity of his patriotic illustrations, Lincoln called Nast "our best recruiting sergeant," but today he is remembered mainly for his classic illustrations of Santa Claus that became popular after the war.

Across Jerome Avenue from the cemetery is Van Cortlandt Park, one of the largest parks in The Bronx. In 1902, the National Guard Association of New York State unveiled a statue of Gen. Josiah Porter (1830–1894) sculpted by William Clark Noble. Porter was one of the first Harvard graduates to enlist in the Union army and commanded the 22nd Regiment of the New York National Guard. The statue, which stands near the Van Cortlandt House Museum, represents Porter in full dress uniform with hat in hand.

Brooklyn

128. FORT HAMILTON, FORT HAMILTON PARK, AND THE HARBOR DEFENSE MUSEUM

230 Sheridan Loop, Brooklyn. Hours: M–F 10:00 a.m. – 4:00 p.m., Sat 10:00 a.m. – 2:00 p.m. General information: www.harbordefensemuseum.com or (718) 630-4349.

Harbor Defense Museum, Fort Hamilton.

Although construction on Fort Hamilton began on April 26, 1825, and it was completed in 1831, the fort never saw action in any conflict. Built to guard the entrance to New York Harbor, it continued to do so until the Second World War; by that time, rifled cannon capable of breaching even thick masonry walls had long since made this type of fortification obsolete. Fort Hamilton was originally designed to house 80 heavy guns in its large casemates, mainly to protect the Narrows from enemy warships. Following the Civil War, Fort Hamilton was converted for other purposes. Wooden barracks were built to house troops, and the old fortification was converted into an officers club. The shape of the fort was also altered over the years; it is now shaped like the letter C. In 1861, the post commander was Capt. Abner Doubleday (1819-1893). Doubleday is perhaps most famous for his supposed invention of the sport of baseball; popular myth has given him the honor despite the fact that he did not invent the game and never claimed he had. Doubleday was second in command at Fort Sumter in Charleston Harbor, South Carolina, and fired the first shot in the Union's 1861 defense of the fortress. He fought bravely at Antietam and Gettysburg.

The Harbor Defense Museum is located in the old caponier, a freestanding bastion originally used to protect the rear of the fort from attack by land. It displays many military objects from the fort's long history, including the Civil War era. The museum is in a section of the fort that is unchanged, although other parts of the large facility have been modernized. Inside the fort is the house where Robert E. Lee (1807–1870) lived during his posting to the fort as engineer from 1841 to 1846. It is somewhat surprising for Northerners to learn that Lee, after completing his education at West Point, began his military career at Fort Hamilton. Another famous Southern general, Thomas "Stonewall" Jackson (1824–1863), was stationed here for two years beginning in 1848. On the grounds are examples of Civil War weaponry, including an Ames 6-pounder (the standard smoothbore fieldpiece) as well as a muzzle fragment from a Confederate 6-pounder that was struck by a Union shell. Several larger guns are currently on display as well. The prototype 20-inch Rodman gun, which was the largest gun in the world in 1864, is located just outside the main entrance to the fort in Fort Hamilton Park.

A stunning example of a Rodman artillery piece.

129. ST. JOHN'S EPISCOPAL CHURCH
9818 Fort Hamilton Parkway, Brooklyn. Hours: T–F 9:00 a.m. – 1:00 p.m., Sunday worship at 10:00 a.m. General information: www.saintjohns1834.org or (718) 745-2377.

The little St. John's Episcopal Church was founded in 1834 for officers stationed at nearby Fort Hamilton. For that reason it has become known as the "Church of the Generals." Robert E. Lee was a vestryman at the church from 1842 to 1844 while posted to the fort. In front of St. John's at 99th Street and Fort Hamilton Parkway stands a tree with a commemorative plaque reading: "This tree was planted by General Robert Edward Lee while stationed at Fort Hamilton from 1842-1847. The tree has been restored and this tablet placed upon it by the New York Chapter, United Daughters of the Confederacy, April 1912." In the 1930s, a new tree was planted; the plaque remains, updated to indicate the replaced tree.

Stonewall Jackson was baptized at St. John's on April 29, 1849. The baptismal font is still in use today. Few know that he was a devout Christian as well as an exceptional general. General Henry Warner Slocum, the Union general who was severely wounded at the first battle of Bull Run, also worshipped here, as did Civil War generals Henry J. Hunt, John Sedgwick, Loomis Langdon, Harvey Brown, and Joseph Bailey.

St. John's Episcopal Church.

130. GREEN-WOOD CEMETERY [COMMONLY GREENWOOD]
Fifth Avenue and 25th Street, Brooklyn. Hours: M–F 8:00 a.m. – 4:00 p.m., Sat 8:00 a.m. – 3:30 p.m. General information: www.green-wood.com or (718) 768-7300.

Green-Wood is New York's largest cemetery, consisting of 478 acres of hills, valleys, and ponds. Nearly a half million graves cover this section of Brooklyn, and the cemetery attracts large groups of visitors who come to admire the nineteenth- and twentieth-century memorials and mausoleums while strolling through the park-like setting.

For anyone interested in the Civil War, the Soldier's Monument is a good place to begin a tour. Ask for a map at the main entrance. This 35-foot-tall granite column was officially dedicated in 1869 and underwent a complete restoration in 2002. Surrounding the column are four freestanding, life-size figures of soldiers representing the army's artillery, cavalry, infantry, and engineering divisions. The monument was erected to honor the more than 150,000 New Yorkers who volunteered for duty during the war. It sits on the highest point in Green-Wood, which is called Battle Hill. (The hill was the site of George Washington's lookout on August 27, 1776, during the battle of Long Island. Near the Civil War Soldier's Monument is the Altar of Liberty, which is dedicated to that Revolutionary War battle.)

Scattered throughout the cemetery are the graves of 18 Civil War generals, including Maj. Gen. Henry Halleck, and 4,500 lower-ranking veterans of that war. At least two of the graves honor Confederate generals, Robert Selden Garnett and Nathaniel Harrison Harris. They are

Major General Henry Halleck's grave.

interred with members of their Northern families, indicating just how divisive the war really was, with brother pitted against brother.

Among the more interesting tombstones is a tall shaft surmounted by an eagle dedicated to "Colonel Abraham Vosburgh of the 71st Infantry Regiment of the New York State Guard." He

Soldier's Monument in Green-Wood Cemetery.

was the first commander of the 71st and proudly marched his 380 men down Broadway in answer to Lincoln's initial call for troops. Vosburgh became one of the earliest casualties of the war when he died on May 20, 1861. Lincoln is said to have placed a wreath on his coffin before it left Washington on its final journey north. In another section is the tomb of William Moir Smith, who died at the first battle of Bull Run. His monument includes a rendering of his hat, kit bag, and a symbolic broken branch, all carved in stone. The headstone for Clarence McKenzie, a 12-year-old drummer boy who was killed in 1861 when a gun accidentally discharged, is made of zinc. McKenzie had the distinction of being the first person from Brooklyn to die during the war.

Among the many noncombatants from the Civil War era buried here are abolitionist minister Henry Ward Beecher, philanthropist Peter Cooper, lithographers Nathaniel Currier and James Merritt Ives, inventor Samuel Morse, architect James Renwick, Jr., editors Horace Greeley and James Gordon Bennett, and jeweler Charles Lewis Tiffany. The cemetery offers many tours, some of which focus on the Civil War monuments.

131. LINCOLN STATUE
Concert Grove in Prospect Park, Brooklyn

The statue of Abraham Lincoln in Prospect Park is one of three dedicated to the martyred president in public parks around the city. This one is a larger-than-life bronze by Henry Kirke Brown, the same sculptor who created the Lincoln figure now in Manhattan's Union Square. Prospect Park's likeness of Lincoln was the second that Brown created (Union Square's was the first), but it was the earliest to be unveiled. As such, it became the very first outdoor statue to honor Lincoln in America. It was dedicated on October 21, 1869, and paid for through a grass-roots effort by nearly 13,000 local donors, none of whom paid more than a dollar each. Originally the statue stood in Grand Army Plaza, but in 1896, when the Soldiers' and Sailors' Memorial Arch was erected there, this statue was moved to Concert Grove. The statue is currently in a part of the park undergoing restoration, and city officials are debating whether to return the statue to Grand Army Plaza.

Statue of Abraham Lincoln (back side).

132. GRAND ARMY PLAZA
Main entrance to Prospect Park on Flatbush Avenue at Eastern Parkway, Brooklyn

Grand Army Plaza covers 11 acres at the entrance to Brooklyn's large Prospect Park. The oval plaza was designed from 1867 to 1870 by the creators of Central Park: Frederick Law Olmsted and Calvert Vaux, and was originally called Prospect Park Plaza. It was intended to be a majestic entrance to the park, and originally sported trees and a peaceful fountain. Renamed Grand Army Plaza in 1926, it has become a busy and noisy traffic circle. In 1885, Seth Low, the mayor of Brooklyn, suggested that a Soldiers' and Sailors' Memorial Arch be erected to honor the

Grand Army Plaza.

Abraham Lincoln relief on the Soldiers' and Sailors' Arch.

sacrifice made by Brooklyn's Civil War troops. Between 1889 and 1892, the 80-foot-tall arch was built following a design that resembles the Arc de Triomphe in Paris and the Arch of Titus in Rome. The architect of the arch was John H. Duncan, the same man who designed Grant's tomb in Manhattan. The grand arch is supported by massive piers rich in architectural detail. Philip Martiny (1858–1927) was hired to provide bas-relief sculptures for the surface of the arch's spandrels.

After the arch was completed, Stanford White of the architectural firm of McKim, Mead and White redesigned the entire plaza and commissioned Frederick MacMonnies (1863–1937) to design three additional sculptures for the plaza. These are the *Quadriga*, *The Spirit of the Army*, and *The Spirit of the Navy*. Next the designers created four Doric columns, each topped with a gigantic bronze bald eagle. Atop the arch, the *Quadriga* depicts Lady Columbia, an allegory for America. She is joined by a two-horse chariot and two other horses held by winged Victory figures reminiscent of Berlin's Brandenburg Gate. In 1901, the bronze high-relief panels were added; they depict idealized army and navy themes. The dedication over the arch reads, "To the Defenders of the Union 1861-65."

On the inside of the arch are relief sculptures of Lincoln and Grant by artist William O'Donovan. Both heroes sit astride horses sculpted by Thomas Eakins, Lincoln with his characteristic stovepipe hat in hand. Between the columns on the arch are medallions for each of the Army and Navy units in which Brooklyn soldiers were active. The military theme continues with a motif of weapons decorating the spiral staircase inside the monument itself, but that area is seldom open to the public.

More statuary has been added to the plaza, including a statue of Gen. Kemble Warren (1830–1882), a hero of the battle of Gettysburg. He is credited with saving the strategic positions on Round Top and Little Round Top during the engagement. The pedestal incorporates actual stones from Little Round Top and was created by Henry Bearer (1837–1908). On the other side of the arch from General Warren, the Gen. Henry Warner Slocum Monument can be seen, now awaiting restoration. Slocum (1827–1894) was a West Point graduate who distinguished himself at first Bull Run and Gettysburg before joining Sherman on his March to the Sea campaign. The equestrian figure shows Slocum with his sword raised in victory. The sculptor of the Slocum monument was Frederick MacMonnies, who also created the statues on the arch itself.

Statue of General Kemble Warren.

133. BROOKLYN MUSEUM
200 Eastern Parkway, Brooklyn. Hours: W–F 10:00 a.m. – 5:00 p.m., Sat–Sun 11:00 a.m. – 6:00 p.m. General information: www.brooklynmuseum.org or (718) 638-5000. Admission charge.

One of New York City's great treasures is the Brooklyn Museum, which is housed in an elegant beaux arts building. It is one of the largest museums in the country and contains many exhibits of interest to the Civil War enthusiast. In addition to decorative and utilitarian objects from the period, the American Art Collection contains important works such as Alexander Pope's wonderful still-life painting entitled "Emblems of the Civil War." Nearby, Eastman Johnson's "A Ride for Liberty – The Fugitive Slaves" of 1862 can be found, as well as his study for "The Wounded Drummer Boy" created just two years later. Brooklyn's famous abolitionist minister Henry Ward Beecher is portrayed on canvas by artist George Augustus Baker, Jr. Also

The Brooklyn Museum.

on display is a gilded bronze cast of the figure of Victory that was created by Augustus Saint-Gaudens for the Robert Gould Shaw Memorial, one of the artist's great masterpieces. Although the completed memorial to the first black Union regiment was unveiled in 1897 in front of Boston's State House, the fourth state (or successive version) of the winged Victory can be found here in Brooklyn. Sculptor John Rogers is represented by his impressive piece "The Council of War," which depicts Lincoln in consultation with Gen. U. S. Grant and Secretary of War Edwin M. Stanton. It was mass-produced in plaster and became popular with upper-middle-class Americans shortly after Lincoln's death. An important bust of Lincoln produced by James Gillinder and Sons rounds out the collection. The museum's collection is equally rich in photographs and prints that show many important people and events of the war years.

134. ULYSSES S. GRANT STATUE
Grant Square, Bergen Street and Bedford Avenue, Brooklyn

A larger-than-life bronze equestrian statue of Gen. Ulysses S. Grant by William Ordway Partridge (1861–1930) was given to the city in 1896 and placed here. It was commissioned by the Union Club of Brooklyn and unveiled on what would have been Grant's 74th birthday, directly across the street from a building that was then the club's headquarters. On the clubhouse itself were placed two terracotta portraits of Lincoln and Grant. There is even a neighborhood in southeast Staten Island named Grant City after the famous general, and the Grant City Apartments are located there on Lincoln Avenue. Grant was buried in New York, and more can be learned about him in the description of his tomb (site 115) on Riverside Drive.

Statue of General Grant.

135. WEEKSVILLE (HUNTERFLY ROAD) HOUSES
1698-1708 Bergen Street, between Rochester and Buffalo Roads (1698, 1700, 1702-04, 1706-08 Bergen St.), Brooklyn

Before the Civil War, the area around the Weeksville section of Brooklyn was a free black community where the residents set up their own schools, churches, and shops. They were also quite active in the nationwide fight against slavery. Four of the original frame houses of the period are still here, and a small park-like setting is being developed. The Weeksville Heritage Center at 1698 Bergen Street carries on a series of historic preservation programs at the location. One of the residents was Maj. Martin Delaney, an African-American who worked as a reporter for a Weeksville newspaper called *Freedman's Torchlight* and was also active in the Underground Railroad. The third black female physician in the country was Dr. Susan Smith McKinney-Steward, who was born in Weeksville in 1847. Another early resident was Moses R. Cobb, born a slave in North Carolina. It is said that he walked from that state to New York following emancipation and became a policeman. During the Draft Riots in 1863, this area became a safe haven for blacks fleeing the racist mobs of the city.

Weeksville houses.

136. CYPRESS HILLS NATIONAL CEMETERY
625 Jamaica Avenue, Brooklyn. Hours: Daily 8:00 a.m. – 4:30 p.m. General information: www.cem.va.gov/cems/nchp/cypresshills.asp or (631) 454-4949.

More than 3,000 soldiers who died of disease and battle injuries in New York City hospitals were interred at Cypress Hills National Cemetery during the Civil War. A report issued in 1870 indicated that by that time 3,170 Union soldiers and 461 Confederate soldiers had been buried here. Today this cemetery covers more than 18 acres and has been expanded to include veterans of other wars. Now more than 21,000 graves dot the landscape. Of particular interest is the Ringgold Monument, a large obelisk erected by soldiers who served under Col. Benjamin Ringgold in the 103rd Regiment at Antietam and Fredericksburg. He was killed in battle on May 3, 1863, and his remains lay in state for two days at the Governor's Room in City Hall before burial. The graves of several Medal of Honor winners are also here, including that of Coxswain John Cooper, who was awarded the medal on two separate occasions; Sgt. Valentine Rossbach; Pvt. John Schiller; QM Edward S. Martin; and Pvt. James Webb, who received the country's highest medal for his heroic action at the second battle of Bull Run. More than half of the Confederate burials represent those men who died in the prisoner-of-war camp on Hart Island (site 157) during the final months of the Civil War.

Also buried in the Cypress Hills Cemetery is the notorious Capt. Nathaniel Gordon, the only slave trader to be hung in American history. In August 1860, Gordon was the captain of the *Erie*, a slave ship that was apprehended illegally carrying 897 slaves, mostly children, from West Africa to the United States. After being found guilty at trial, Gordon was scheduled to be executed

Cypress Hills National Cemetery.

on February 21, 1862. The night before his execution Gordon tried to cheat the hangman by committing suicide with strychnine, but was unsuccessful and was hung in the courtyard of Manhattan's Tombs prison on Centre Street as planned. The body was taken to Cypress Hills Cemetery and buried in an unmarked grave on hillside lot 403, section 4, grave 13.

137. GENERAL EDWARD FOWLER STATUE
Junction of Fulton and Lafayette Streets and South Elliott Place, Brooklyn

Although Brig. Gen. Edward Fowler (1828–1896) was mistakenly reported to have been killed at the first battle of Bull Run, he lived to command troops in 22 major Civil War battles. The men under him were known as the "Red-Legged Devils" due to the red puttees they strapped to their legs. Sculptor Henry Bearer created this monument for the community in 1902, six years after Fowler finally passed away. Fowler had been born and raised in Brooklyn and was one of her

Statue of General Edward Fowler.

most esteemed citizens. In 1896, his body lay in state in Brooklyn's Borough Hall before being buried in Green-Wood Cemetery. This monument was originally placed in Fort Greene Park, but after the statue underwent restoration in 1975 it was moved to the present location in this small park, closer to where Fowler lived for nearly 60 years.

138-139. HENRY WARD BEECHER STATUE and LINCOLN'S GETTYSBURG ADDRESS TABLET
Cadman Plaza, in front of Brooklyn Borough Hall, Brooklyn

Following Henry Ward Beecher's death in 1887, a committee was set up to raise money to erect a monument in his honor. The members commissioned the great artist John Quincy Adams Ward to sculpt an 8-foot-tall likeness of the abolitionist pastor of the Plymouth Church. The noted architect Richard Morris Hunt was hired to design the pedestal. Inscribed on the base are the words "Great Apostle of the Brotherhood of Man." The grouping includes not only Beecher but three children, two white, one black. When the statue was dedicated on June 24, 1891, more than 15,000 people crowded the park in front of Borough Hall. In 1959, the statue was moved a short distance to the present site on Cadman Plaza.

Mounted on the wall of the old Borough Hall itself is a bronze tablet inscribed with the full text of Lincoln's immortal Gettysburg Address. Many public schools around the country display the famous speech, but this outdoor marker on a courthouse is unusual. Dedicated in 1909, it includes a likeness of Lincoln in bas-relief. A similar bronze tablet with the text was unveiled a year earlier at Newton High School, 48-01 90th Street in Elmhurst, Queens.

Gettysburg Address tablet.

Statue of Henry Ward Beecher.

140. BROOKLYN HISTORICAL SOCIETY
128 Pierrepont Street, Brooklyn. Hours: W–F 12:00 p.m. – 5:00 p.m.,
Sat 10:00 a.m. – 5:00 p.m., Sun 12:00 p.m. – 5:00 p.m. General information:
www.brooklynhistory.org or (718) 222-4111. Admission charge.

The Brooklyn Historical Society's museum and library contains a wealth of information
relating to this borough's activities during the Civil War. Their holdings include correspondence,
diaries, and scrapbooks of many Union and Confederate soldiers as well as regimental papers,
muster rolls, and other documents. These include the papers of Gen. Wlodzmierz Krzyzanowski
(the commander of the Polish Legion), Maj. Gen. Edward Molineux, and Rear Adm. John

Brooklyn Historical Society.

Lorimer Worden (the commander of the U.S.S. *Monitor*), as well as material related to that ship and its crew. The library also has an original reward poster for the capture of John Wilkes Booth and a fine collection of broadsides, recruiting posters, and photographs available for research. The records of Plymouth Church (see next entry) held by the society contain the sermons and eulogies of Henry Ward Beecher, a signed copy of the "Battle Hymn of the Republic" by Julia Ward Howe, and a letter from Robert Todd Lincoln, the president's only surviving son.

141. PLYMOUTH CHURCH and HENRY WARD BEECHER STATUE
Orange Street between Henry and Hicks Streets, Brooklyn. Hours and general information: www.plymouthchurch.org or (718) 403-9546.

When Abraham Lincoln came to New York City in 1860 as a relatively unknown Illinois politician, the only church services he attended were at Henry Ward Beecher's parish in Brooklyn, the Plymouth Church. In those days, Beecher (1813–1887) was well known as a dynamic New England abolitionist minister, and his sermons attracted enormous crowds every week. Beecher arrived in Brooklyn in 1847 to serve as pastor of this church. Soon after his arrival

Plymouth Church.

Statue of Henry Ward Beecher and Abraham Lincoln Memorial.

the church burnt down, so he launched a building project that was completed in January 1850. The new church, which still stands, was able to hold 2,800 congregants, and each Sunday for the next 40 years Beecher had no trouble filling those seats. Beecher delivered one of his most famous sermons on February 5, 1860, during which he auctioned off a nine-year-old black slave girl named "Pinky" to illustrate the immorality of slavery. The congregation raised $900 to buy her freedom. She was baptized and given the name Rose Ward by Reverend Beecher. (In May 1927, Rose Ward Hunt, by then in her 70s, returned to Plymouth Church to tell a new generation about her life on the occasion of the 80th anniversary of the church.) Just a few weeks after Beecher's slave auction, Abraham Lincoln attended services here. Lincoln had been invited to speak at Plymouth in November 1859 but had been unable to keep that date. He suggested February 1860 as an alternative, and in the interim the venue was changed to the new Cooper Union Great Hall in Manhattan. The telegram asking Lincoln to speak is now part of the collection at the New York Historical Society, while a copy is kept at the church. The pew where Lincoln sat on February 26, 1860, is identified by a silver marker, and a large relief in the garden commemorates his visit.

Beecher was not only a fiery speaker from the pulpit, he was also a man who took action when necessary. At one point, he sent rifles to Kansas to be used in the fight to keep the state free of slavery. The guns were in boxes labeled "Bibles" and therefore became known in Kansas as "Beecher's Bibles." The Plymouth Church also served as a major stop on the Underground Railroad, funneling runaway slaves to Canada. In 1863, midway through the war, Beecher went on an extended speaking tour of England that helped turn public opinion there in favor of the North. As one of the most charismatic men in America, even Southerners were interested in hearing what Beecher had to say. On the eve of their firebomb attack on the city in 1864, Confederate conspirators Martin and Headley took the ferry to Brooklyn (before the famous bridge was built) to listen to Beecher preach. Following Lee's surrender, Lincoln asked the minister to take part in the ceremonies at Fort Sumter to restore the American flag, but Lincoln himself did not live to see that happen. When Beecher died in 1887, he was buried in Brooklyn's Green-Wood Cemetery.

The bronze statue of Henry Ward Beecher in the churchyard is by Gutzon Borglum, the sculptor who created Mount Rushmore. The group includes two seated slave children. That monument was dedicated in 1914 at ceremonies attended by Beecher's great-grandchildren. Inside the church are other reminders of Beecher's tenure as pastor, during which he was widely considered the most talented evangelist in America. His sister Harriet Beecher Stowe (1811–1896) was a member of the Plymouth Church and is represented in one of the stained glass windows. In 1852, she became as famous as her brother with the publication of her novel *Uncle Tom's Cabin*. That book more than any other helped turn public opinion against the institution of slavery. Take time to admire the beautiful windows in the church dedicated to Beecher, Lincoln, and others. During the war years, Reverend Beecher lived nearby at 124 Columbia Heights; in 1881 he moved in with his son at 124 Hicks Street.

142. WALT WHITMAN HISTORICAL MARKER
28 Old Fulton Street, Brooklyn

Beneath the Brooklyn end of the Brooklyn Bridge is the Eagle Warehouse, the site of a building in which Walt Whitman (1819–1892), one of America's greatest poets, once worked. At the age of eight Whitman arrived in Brooklyn from West Hills, Long Island, after his father gave up farming to become a carpenter. His family lived in a succession of houses that his father built

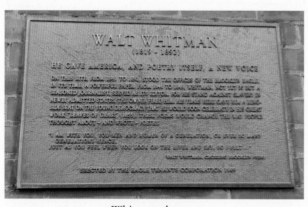

Whitman plaque.

and then sold. Researchers estimate that Whitman lived in nearly a dozen different places in Brooklyn by the time the Civil War began. From 1846 to 1848, he worked as a newspaperman for the *Brooklyn Eagle* whose offices were here. Whitman was fired in large part because of his antislavery stance, a position that was not popular in New York at the time. On one occasion he became so angry with his publisher that he pushed him down the stairs. However, he must have been forgiven, because throughout the war his letters back to Brooklyn from Washington, DC,

were often printed in the *Eagle*. As a staunch Unionist, Whitman wrote some of his best poems about Lincoln and the war. The assassination of the president in 1865 profoundly affected the poet, and he wrote his great poem "O Captain! My Captain!" in Lincoln's memory the same year.

Although Whitman lived in many houses during his early life, surprisingly little has survived. Scholars Paul Berman, Eli Wilentz, and Sean Wilentz have recently discovered that one of the Brooklyn houses built in 1848 and lived in by Whitman's family may still be standing. During Whitman's day the house was listed at 106 Myrtle Street, but today the address is 99 Ryerson Street, where the old house still seems to lurk behind a renovated facade. Recently a small park near Brooklyn's Borough Hall was designated as Walt Whitman Park.

A modern view of the Brooklyn Eagle warehouse.

143. BROOKLYN NAVY YARD
Navy Street, opposite Sands Street, Brooklyn

The 40-acre Brooklyn Navy Yard was established by the federal government in 1801 and used for the construction and refitting of naval vessels. Before the Civil War, the Brooklyn base was second in importance to the one in Norfolk, but when the latter installation fell to the South Brooklyn's became the Union Navy's largest base. During the Civil War, about 6,000 men were employed here 24 hours a day, producing everything from ships to shot. Throughout the war the yards were under the command of Rear Adm. Hiram Paulding (1797–1878), appointed to the post by President Lincoln to build a wartime fleet. Hundreds of merchant ships were converted into cruisers and Paulding oversaw the construction of nearly 20 new vessels. Many of the navy's new ironclads were also serviced here, including the famous *Monitor*.

The yards were used for other purposes as well. Navy recruits were trained on board the *North Carolina*, which was based here permanently. For many of the soon-to-be sailors, it was the first time they had ever been on board a ship. The Navy Yard was also the location for top-secret

A modern view of the Brooklyn Navy Yard.

experiments with a submarine battering ram intended to fire shots while submerged. John Rector also tested his new inflatable life rafts here, filling them with men from the frigate USS *San Jacinto*. They floated around the East River, proving that the gutta percha-based devices would not sink.

Throughout its history, the walls of the Navy Yard were fortified and guns were mounted to protect it against enemy attack. Ironically, however, the only real threat of attack the Navy Yard ever faced came during the Draft Riots in 1863. The mob did not risk approaching, however, because the defenders trained heavy artillery on the main gate. Today many of the old buildings still survive and Civil War structures can be found throughout the grounds.

144. CONTINENTAL IRON WORKS
Waterfront along Calyer, Quay, and Franklin Streets, Greenpoint, Brooklyn

The Navy's first ironclad, the USS *Monitor*, was assembled at Thomas F. Rowland's large Continental Iron Works here in Brooklyn. It was composed of parts made by various manufacturers. To complete the ironclad as quickly as possible, many of the company's 1,500 employees worked day and night on it. Union officers had heard that the Confederate Navy was producing an ironclad of its own to smash the Union's blockade of Richmond and Norfolk, so they needed to work fast to counter that threat. The structural elements of the ship were first laid out in October 1861 and the completed vessel was launched from the yard on January 30, 1862.

Many predicted that the heavy vessel would immediately sink to the bottom of the East River, but the *Monitor* proved to be seaworthy. On March 9 of that year, the *Monitor* engaged the Confederate warship *Merrimack* (or *Virginia*), fighting to a draw in the waters off Hampton Roads, Virginia. The *Monitor*, designed by John Ericsson, would revolutionize naval combat worldwide and signal the end of wooden battleships. Immediately following the first engagement, the Union ordered another seven ironclads from the Continental Iron Works, including the 1,800-ton *Montauk*. With these ships, the North was soon able to take control of all the rivers and harbors in the country. The iron works simultaneously fabricated gun carriages and mortar beds to arm other naval vessels. The Continental Iron Works remained in business at this location from 1851 to 1889. Not far from this location in Greenpoint is Monitor Street, which borders Monsignor McGolrick Park. Within the park is a beautiful bronze memorial dedicated in 1938 by sculptor Antonio de Filippo (1900–1993) that commemorates the battle between the *Monitor* and the *Merrimack*.

Two officers inspect the battered turret of the USS *Monitor*, which suffered several direct hits during its famous battle with the CSS *Virginia* in Hampton Roads.

Officers of the USS *Monitor*.

Queens

145. CALVARY SOLDIERS' MONUMENT

Calvary Cemetery: 49-02 Laurel Hill Boulevard, Woodside, Queens. General information: (718) 786-8000. (Be certain to look for the old Calvary Cemetery, because the larger cemetery consists of several units that stretch for miles along the road.)

The Soldiers' Monument in section 4 of the first Calvary Cemetery was commissioned by the city at the end of the war and completed in 1866. John G. Draddy (1833–1904), well known in New York for his memorials, was selected to do the work at war's end. The 50-foot-tall granite column is decorated with bronze garlands and flags and topped with a figure representing peace holding a cross. Draddy also created the four life-size figures of Civil War soldiers, one for each of the divisions of the Union army (artillery, cavalry, infantry, and engineering). Three years later he

Calvary Soldiers' Monument detail.

Calvary Soldiers' Monument.

would duplicate the same four figures in stone for the Civil War Soldiers' Monument in Brooklyn's Green-Wood Cemetery; here they are in the original bronze, and in more recent years one has been restored. Originally there were also four cannon at the corners, surrounded by a typical iron fence of the period, but these were subsequently removed.

Next to the monument is the grave of Tipperary-born Col. Timothy O'Meara. He was a member of the "Tammany Regiment" as well as the "Jackson Guards." At the battle of Ball's Bluff in October 1861, he was taken prisoner but was later exchanged for Confederate soldiers. After seeing action with Grant in the Vicksburg and Jackson campaigns, he died of wounds received in battle at Missionary Ridge in Chattanooga, Tennessee, on November 25, 1863. Within the cemetery, one of the largest in the United States, are the graves of many other Roman Catholic Union soldiers, including Gens. Francis Herron and Eliakim Scammon and two Medal of Honor recipients.

146. SOLDIERS' AND SAILORS' MONUMENT
Hillside Avenue and 173rd Street, Queens

In 1896, artist Frederick Wellington Ruckstuhl's beaux arts memorial to Civil War soldiers and sailors was unveiled in Queens. The 10-foot-tall monument depicts an angel holding a wreath to symbolize victory and a palm bough for strength. The monument, intended as a sign of peace, commemorates the Union soldiers from Queens who died during the war. In 1958, this monument was moved here from Merrick Boulevard due to traffic congestion there. Later Ruckstuhl used this same Angel of Peace to pay homage to the South Carolina Women of the Confederacy. Today that statue stands on the grounds of the South Carolina statehouse in Columbia.

Soldiers' and Sailors' Monument.

147. QUEENS HISTORICAL SOCIETY

Historic Kingsland Homestead, 143-135 37th Avenue, Flushing, Queens. Hours: T, Sat, Sun 2:30 p.m. – 4:30 p.m. General information: www.queens historicalsociety.org or (718) 939-0647. Admission charge.

The Queens Historical Society operates a small museum that displays the history of this borough. Within its collection are fine examples of Civil War letters to and from Union soldiers, including the correspondence of Edward L. Murray of the 69th New York Regiment. In December 1864, Murray became one of more than 11,700 soldiers who died of camp fever and starvation in the notorious Salisbury (North Carolina) prison. Other Civil War items here include the funeral train timetable produced after the death of Ulysses S. Grant and postwar reunion pamphlets and documentation.

Queens Historical Society.

148. FLUSHING CEMETERY
16306 46th Avenue at 164th Street, Flushing, Queens.
General information: (718) 359-0100

The first soldier from Queens to fall during the Civil War was Cpl. George Huntsman, who is buried in Flushing Cemetery. He was a member of the 5th Regiment New York Volunteers, commonly known as Duryea's Zouaves. They were the colorful soldiers who dressed in Turkish-style uniforms of bright red billowy pants and fezzes. Huntsman, just 19 at the time, died of wounds suffered in the second battle of Bull Run in 1862, and it was in his honor that the George Huntsman Post of the Grand Army of the Republic was named in 1869. Major Jacob Roemer, Flushing's most outstanding Civil War hero, is also buried here. He suffered nine wounds during the 57 engagements in which he participated. Twenty-five other Civil War veterans were laid to rest in Flushing Cemetery, including Pvt. Carl Ludwig, who received the Medal of Honor for his brave and gallant action in the second battle of Petersburg. Simon Baruch is also buried in Flushing Cemetery; the write-up on Baruch Place (site 038) contains reference to him as an assistant surgeon who served in the Confederate army with the 3rd South Carolina Infantry Battalion.

George Huntsman's grave.

149. CAPTAIN WILLIAM DERMODY MONUMENT
48th Avenue and 216th Street, Bayside, Queens

Captain William Dermody was with the 67th Regiment New York Volunteers. When he died during the fighting at Spotsylvania in 1864, he became the first soldier to die in the Civil War from Bayside, another Queens neighborhood. His sister set aside ground as a memorial for her fallen brother on what was farmland at the time. A school was built on the site in his honor and two trees were planted, a maple for the North and a sycamore for the South. Over the years the trees

grew to maturity and died and the schoolhouse was torn down. In 1935, new trees were planted and a boulder that remains there to this day was added, but even that modest memorial has been neglected and vandalized. At one time there was a bronze plaque attached to the boulder, but that disappeared long ago. On the memorial boulder that sits in the center of Captain Dermody Triangle is the lone inscription: "For A Better Union 1861-1865." Captain Dermody is the first of many soldiers listed on the Flushing Civil War Monument, which was erected in 1865 at the intersection of Northern Boulevard and Linden Place in front of the Flushing Town Hall.

Captain William Dermody monument.

150. FORT TOTTEN BATTERY
Cross Island Parkway off Totten Avenue, Willets Point, Queens. Open daily.

Fort Totten was constructed by William Petit Trowbridge between 1862–1864 directly across the straits from Fort Schuyler. Together the two forts made an excellent defense for the city from attack through Long Island Sound. Although construction of the fort began in 1862, it was not named Fort Totten until 1898. Military use of the fort ended in 1974 and much of the area is now a public park. The visitor center houses a museum that displays the history of the fort. The former Fort Totten officers club is now the home of the Bayside Historical Society. The building was probably designed by Robert E. Lee before the war when he was a U.S. Army engineer stationed nearby at Fort Hamilton; however, other scholars believe that Lee merely approved the drawings of a subordinate and didn't design the building himself.

The battery was part of the seacoast fortifications designed by Joseph E. Totten, the chief army engineer from 1838 until his death in 1864, and is named in his honor. The system he developed included the brick- and stonework as well as the vaulted rooms for the gun emplacements. Massive, thick walls were needed to withstand naval bombardment at the time, but newer, rifled artillery quickly made this type of fortification obsolete. During the Civil War the fort was used for training and weapon storage by the Union army, and saw no action.

(Top) Fort Totten Officer's Club;
(Below) Fort Totten Battery, ca. 1915.

Fort Totten, Long Island, N. Y.

74-25

Staten Island

151. STATEN ISLAND HISTORICAL SOCIETY and HISTORIC RICHMOND TOWN
441 Clarke Avenue, Staten Island. Hours: W–Sun 1:00 p.m. – 5:00 p.m.
General information: www.historicrichmondtown.org or (718) 351-1611.

Historic Richmond Town is an old village and museum complex that allows visitors to roam through buildings and enjoy exhibits illustrating life from all periods of the city's history, including the Civil War. Sprawling over 50 acres in the center of Staten Island, the museum features 30 different buildings. One of them is the Third County Courthouse, which served as the courthouse for Richmond County during the Civil War, long before Staten Island was

Third County Courthouse.

incorporated into New York City. In July 1863, the unrest of the city's draft riots spilled over into neighboring towns and a small military detachment from nearby Camp Sprague in New Dorp was called out to protect a black man who was imprisoned in the Richmond Town courthouse. Today the building has been restored to look as it did during that period.

Resting on the ground to the left of the Treasure House in Richmond Town sits an 1857 Dahlgren naval cannon used during the Civil War on the three-masted, steam-screw frigate USS *Colorado*. The *Colorado* saw action as the Union's flagship for the blockade squadron that patrolled the Atlantic Coast from New York to New Orleans. This cannon was recovered from the sea in the area near Fort Lafayette; it must have been discarded when the ship was cut up for scrap in 1885. Other Civil War treasures in the Staten Island Historical Society's collection include the papers of Brig. Gen. Alfred Napoleon Duffie, Lt. Col. William G. Ward, Capt. David Stothers, and the abolitionist Sydney Howard Gay. All these are located in the Society's archives and available for research.

152. FORT RICHMOND, NOW CALLED BATTERY WEED, and FORTS TOMPKINS AND WADSWORTH
Hudson Road, Staten Island. Hours: W–Sun 10:00 a.m. – 4:30 p.m.
General information: (718) 354-4500.

Battery Weed.

Battery Weed is now part of the Fort Wadsworth Military Reservation and is open to the public as a museum. It was built between 1849 and 1861 as Fort Richmond to guard the Narrows, the gateway to New York Harbor from the Atlantic Ocean. It is located strategically across from Fort Hamilton, which is on the Brooklyn side of the channel. Like Fort Totten, it was designed by Gen. Joseph G. Totten (1788–1864) and later named for Gen. Stephen Weed (1831–1863), who had been killed at the battle of Gettysburg. The fort is in the shape of a trapezoid, with three tiers of guns housed under open arches. During the Civil War, it boasted approximately 116 guns, making it the strongest fortification along the Atlantic coast.

Fort Tompkins was built between 1861 and 1870 and stands on the crest of the hill above Battery Weed. It was finished too late to see much Civil War activity, and was used primarily as a barracks for Battery Weed. Both Battery Weed and Fort Tompkins are good examples of the type of heavy granite masonry fortifications that were rendered useless by the new rifled cannon developed during the Civil War era. Fort Wadsworth, beneath the bridge at Bay Street and Wadsworth Avenue, has the distinction of being the oldest continually staffed military reservation in America, having first been used for military purposes in 1663. In 1865, it was renamed in honor of Brevet Maj. Gen. James Samuel Wadsworth (1807–1864), who had been killed during the battle of the Wilderness the previous year.

Fort Tompkins.

If you visit Staten Island via the Staten Island ferry, take time to visit the memorial erected in 1915 to the memory of Maj. Clarence T. Barrett. It is in Barrett Triangle, the park bounded by Hyatt Street, Bay Street, Stuyvesant Place, and Richmond Terrace. Barrett signed on with the 175th New York at the outbreak of the war and took part in the Union's 1864 siege of Mobile and the final battles around Richmond that ended the war. The classical bronze figure of a warrior by artist Sherry Edmundson Fry stands on a pedestal decorated with traditional Greek figures and the motto "Loyal, Honest, Brave and True."

Other Islands

153. FORT LAFAYETTE
Once on an island that is underneath the east pier of the Verrazano Bridge

Fort Lafayette, called the "Bastille of the North," was one of the massive coastal fortifications built to defend New York City from attack by sea. This island fort was about 400 yards offshore from what is now Bay Ridge, Brooklyn. The fort was begun during the War of 1812 and completed in 1818 as Fort Diamond, later to be renamed in honor of the Marquis de La Fayette. Until 1861, the fort sported 72 cannon that guarded the harbor, but it was converted to a prison during the Civil War and housed Confederate soldiers as well as spies and political prisoners. In 1868, the fort burned and was not rebuilt.

Early in his administration, President Lincoln suspended the writ of *habeas corpus*, and many suspected secessionists were incarcerated at Fort Lafayette without trial. In the old brick fort, the conditions varied according to the reporter. Some suspected that the commanding officer, Lt. Col. Martin Burke, favored the Confederates detained here, since his family came from the border state

Fort Lafayette, ca. 1915.

of Maryland. Reports do indicate that he was harshest on the Union prisoners. However, when stories about the easy treatment of Southerners appeared in New York newspapers, the public was outraged—so Burke cracked down on all prisoners equally. In 1861, when Lincoln had some members of the Maryland Legislature arrested so they could not vote on secession from the Union, they were detained here. Although they shared their cramped quarters with cannon, they were well provided for and enjoyed good food, liquor, and furniture. Southerners who had been caught trying to run the Union blockade were not as lucky: they were chained to the walls.

Many notable political figures spent time in this prison, including the mayor of Baltimore, George William Brown; the editor of the *Baltimore Republic*, Beale Richardson; and Gen. William Fitzhugh Lee, Robert E. Lee's son. One Union general, Charles Stone, who had commanded troops at Ball's Bluff in 1861, was imprisoned here for two months without being charged. Some believed he was a traitor and had met with the enemy before the battle to deliver secrets, but no

Landing prisoners at Fort Lafayette, 1861.

betrayal was ever proven. After the war, Stone lived in self-imposed exile in Egypt. He returned to New York Harbor in the 1880s to work as an engineer, preparing the pedestal for the Statue of Liberty.

Robert Cobb Kennedy, one of the Confederate conspirators who tried to burn down New York City by setting fire to a dozen hotels in November 1864, was eventually captured and detained at Fort Lafayette, where, true to form, he attempted to set fire to his cell. There, on March 25, 1865, he was hanged before a large crowd. Some members of the public paid as much as $50 for a ticket to view the execution. Press coverage at the time mentioned that the gallows did not work correctly, so it took Kennedy a half hour to die at the end of a rope. He was buried in the cemetery at Fort Hamilton, but later his family removed the body to an unknown location somewhere in Brooklyn. Another of the conspirators, Lt. Col. Robert Martin, was also sent to Fort Lafayette to stand trial, but he was released in February 1866. Martin later moved to Brooklyn, where he operated a tobacco warehouse. When he died in 1901, he was buried in Brooklyn's Green-Wood Cemetery.

154. GOVERNORS ISLAND
New York Harbor, by ferry from Battery Park. Hours: F 10:00 a.m. – 5:00 p.m., Sat–Sun 10:00 a.m. – 7:00 p.m. General information: www.govisland.com or (212) 440-2200.

Castle Williams, ca. 1911.

During the Civil War, the military facilities on Governors Island were used not only to protect the harbor but as a base of supply for the forts along the East Coast, including those forts deep within enemy territory. The island served as an operations headquarters and a prison as well. Governors Island is much larger than it looks: it covers 172 acres. On the island is a wide variety of buildings, some dating back over 200 years. Castle Williams, built between 1807 and 1811, is in the shape of a sandstone circle 200 feet in diameter. It was pressed into service as a prison for nearly 700 Confederate enlisted men, while nearby Fort Jay (renamed Fort Columbus during the Civil War period) held Confederate officers. Castle Williams was also where a firing squad executed the bounty jumper James Devlin in 1865. He had been found guilty of joining at least three different regiments to collect the enlistment bonuses, each time deserting the unit as soon as he had his money. The basement of a building near Fort Jay held the most dangerous spies who had already been convicted or were awaiting trial. Throughout the course of the war, the island was also used to process thousands of volunteer and conscripted men prior to their assignment to duty. Also on the island is the Block House, a brick Greek Revival building built in the early 1840s that has served as a hospital, prison, and officers' quarters. A young lieutenant by the name of Ulysses S. Grant lived here from April to July of 1852. He liked the fresh sea air on the island and wrote to his wife that the location made it easy to get to the city whenever he wanted. To the south of the Block House is the Episcopal Chapel of St. Cornelius the Centurion. In the nave are many battle and regimental flags, including the one that Gen. Philip Sheridan carried in the battle of Five Forks in April 1865.

In 1861, the government commissioned the steamship *The Star of the West* to take supplies from Governors Island to Fort Sumter in Charleston Harbor to relieve the siege it was then under. The ship was one of many that Cornelius Vanderbilt made available for use by the military at a rate reported to be somewhere between $10,000 and $30,000 a month. When *The Star of the West*

Fort Jay, ca. 1900.

reached the mouth of Charleston Harbor on January 9, 1861, she was fired upon by the cadets at The Citadel, a military academy overlooking the harbor. After the ship was hit three times, it turned around without accomplishing its mission and returned to Governors Island. In effect, these were the first shots fired in what was to become the Civil War.

In 1865, just days before the end of the war, one Confederate prisoner, Capt. William Robert Webb, could stand imprisonment on Governors Island no longer, so he swam to freedom. When he finally pulled himself out of the water at the Battery, no one believed he was an escaped prisoner, so he was able to make his way safely back to Tennessee.

155. FORT WOOD, NOW LIBERTY ISLAND
New York Harbor, by ferry from Battery Park. Hours: Daily 8:30 a.m. – 6:15 p.m. General information: www.nps.gov/stli or (212) 363-3200. Admission charge.

Fort Wood was the name given to the fortifications on Bedloe's Island in 1814. It was named for Lt. Col. Eleazer Wood (1783–1814), who had been killed at the battle of Fort Erie in Canada during the War of 1812. It was not until the Statue of Liberty was constructed here in 1886 that Bedloe's Island became known as Liberty Island. Fort Wood's massive stone walls (in the shape of an 11-pointed star) were converted into the base for Lady Liberty. During much of the Civil War, Fort Wood was used as a supply and weapons depot. One interesting footnote is that on July 13, 1860, the last man executed for piracy in America, Albert Hicks, was hung by the neck on Bedloe's Island in front of a crowd of nearly 10,000 people.

Postcard view of the Statue of Liberty, ca. 1965.

156. FORT GIBSON, NOW ELLIS ISLAND
New York Harbor, by ferry from Battery Park. Hours: Daily 8:30 a.m. – 6:15 p.m. General information: www.nps.gov/elis or (212) 363-3200. Admission charge.

Only a small section of Fort Gibson, which was built on tiny Oyster Island, remains. It can be seen outside the Immigration Museum on what is now known as Ellis Island. Originally Fort Gibson was designed to be nothing more than a battery of artillery hastily erected to defend the harbor during the War of 1812. It was named in honor of Col. James Gibson who, like Eleazer Wood (see Fort Wood, site 155), had been killed at the battle of Fort Erie. The 3-tier, 20-gun battery was not needed during the Civil War, so it was dismantled in 1861 and the guns sent elsewhere. The barracks and ammunition supply depot remained until the island was taken over as a federal immigration station in 1892. At that time, land was reclaimed from the harbor, more than doubling the size of the island and obliterating the military facilities. It was only recently that excavations uncovered the fort's foundation stones.

157. HART ISLAND, DAVIDS ISLAND, AND FORT SLOCUM
Long Island Sound, off the coast of the Bronx. Restricted access.

The federal government bought a portion of Hart Island in the 1860s to serve as a military training ground. Here more than 50,000 Union troops went through basic training. Notably, three black infantry units drilled here. Today this island serves as New York's potter's field, where nearly a million homeless and destitute people have been buried. During the Civil War, many of the recruits who died of disease during training were also buried here. A 16-foot-tall obelisk was

Landing Dock at Fort Slocum, ca. 1916.

erected in their memory. During the twentieth century, their remains were transferred to other military cemeteries. In the final days of the Civil War, Hart Island also served as a prisoner of war camp. A total of 3,413 captured Confederate soldiers were held here; of those, 235 died in the camp. Their remains were originally interred on the island, but in 1941 they were moved to the Cypress Hills National Cemetery in Brooklyn.

In 1862, De Camp General Hospital was set up on Davids Island, a small island next to Hart Island, to treat Union casualties. Later in the war, the facilities were expanded to accommodate wounded Confederate prisoners as well. Twenty-two buildings were erected quickly to house up to 2,500 patients at a time, but after the war the treatment center was downsized. In 1896, the medical installation on the island was renamed Fort Slocum in honor of Civil War Gen. Henry Warner Slocum. The base was abandoned in 1966, and recently the island was given to the city of New Rochelle to convert to recreational purposes.

Officer's Row, Fort Slocum, ca. 1913.

Appendix A

Some Significant Events

Some Civil War-period events in New York City took place over a large geographical area, leaving connections to multiple sites. Overall descriptions of a few of those events are given below. Throughout the text sites linked to these events are marked with an asterisk.

1. The Lincolns' Visits to the City

Abraham Lincoln and his wife Mary made their first visit to New York City in July 1857 as tourists. In February 1860, Lincoln stayed at the Astor House Hotel on Broadway when he returned to deliver a speech in Cooper Union's Great Hall. That speech is often cited as the turning point in his political career: it helped propel him to the presidency. While in the city he shopped at Brooks Brothers for a top hat and had his photograph taken by Mathew Brady. On his way to his inauguration the following year, he again stayed at the Astor House, and it became Mary Todd Lincoln's preferred hotel on her famous shopping trips to the city. Although New York State overwhelmingly supported Lincoln, the citizens of New York City voted against him twice. However, after his assassination more than a half million people climbed the steps of City Hall to pay their respects as he lay in state there, before the presidential funeral train took his body back to Illinois.

See entries for sites 009, 010, 012, 013, 021, 023, 028, 035, 049, 051, 054, 066, 067, 083, and 141 for specific information.

2. Draft Riots

By the summer of 1863, the number of volunteers to the army was dwindling, so Lincoln realized he would need to conscript a large number of men. He signed a law calling for a national draft, but the law contained a provision that anyone could buy his way out of military service for $300. This upset those who were too poor to exercise that option. In New York City, Saturday, July 11, 1863, was chosen as the day to begin randomly selecting names via a lottery. A crowd gathered on the sidewalks around the draft office at the corner of Third Avenue and 46th Street, but the police were there in force and there was no trouble. This was not the case when the draft resumed the following Monday morning. By that time the poor Irish immigrants in the city had organized, and widespread violence broke out in many parts of the city. The draft office was burnt to the ground and mobs roamed the city looking for trouble. They looted shops and businesses, and even burnt down churches and the Colored Orphan Asylum. They attacked free black men, hanging some, and attacked the police who were trying in vain to maintain order. On July 16, after several days of rioting, the army was called back from Gettysburg to put down the disturbances, which left more than a hundred people dead.

See entries for sites 007, 016, 021, 031, 041, 043, 055, 066, 069, 073, 075, 076, 085, 092, 094, 097, 098, 109, 122, 135, 143, and 151 for specific information.

3. Confederate Arson Attack

On November 25, 1864, a small group of Confederate conspirators set fire to 13 hotels throughout the city. They hoped the fires would join and create a firestorm that would engulf the city in flames. Their goal was to cause panic and the diversion of Union troops from the battlefield. They also believed that this show of terrorism would cause those in New York City who were sympathetic to the Southern cause to rebel against the government, but it only served to solidify anti-Southern sentiments. The arsonists were poorly trained and ill-equipped, and in the end none of the fires they set did significant damage. Some of the conspirators were captured later, but only one was executed for his crimes.

See entries for sites 009, 010, 016, 022, 031, 035, 054, 065, 076, 083, 141, and 153 for specific information.

Appendix B

An Interview with Author Bill Morgan

Q: *Why did you decide to write your book on this particular topic?*

BM: I have had a life-long interest in the Civil War. Forty years ago I moved to New York City and as I walked around the city, I continually noticed places that had links to the Civil War. I did not live far from the Cooper Union, and was thrilled to find that the very auditorium where Abraham Lincoln gave his first great speech was still there, completely intact. It is often referred to as the speech that made him president, and as I read more I discovered that he had his picture taken the same day at Mathew Brady's studio and might have stopped in McSorley's Tavern for a drink. And both those buildings are still there as well. These discoveries prompted me to start a file of Civil War-related sites around town. Eventually I realized that there were as many Civil War sites in the city as there were on the great battlefields of the war, but no one had ever taken the time to put it all together; so, the book grew out of that activity. Some Civil War-period events in New York City took place over a large geographical area, leaving connections to multiple sites. Overall descriptions of a few of those events are given below.

Q: *What makes your book unique from other books on the same topic?*

BM: Quite honestly, there are no other books on the same topic. In fact, there are a very few books on the role that New York City played in the Civil War, but those generally focus on the Draft Riots of 1863 and seldom do any tour guides list Civil War sites. It seems incredible to me that no one pulled all these locations together before, but I'm pleased to have been the one to do it.

Q: *What are some features of your book that you think readers will really enjoy?*

BM: Obviously, people will be interested to discover some of the little-known facts about New York's role in the war, but they won't have to visit New York City to enjoy learning about them through the pages of this book. Most people can't believe that Robert E. Lee lived in the city for several years and the church he attended is still standing. Stonewall Jackson was also a resident of the city and visited on his honeymoon. Although many know that he was a devout "born again" Christian, they are surprised to learn that he was actually baptized in New York City in a church that is still standing. Mrs. Jefferson Davis moved to New York after her husband's death and found a job as a columnist for the *New York World* newspaper.

Of course everyone is most surprised by the Confederate links to the city, but it shouldn't be surprising if you understand that New Yorkers hated Lincoln and voted against him overwhelmingly in both presidential elections. The upstate Republicans were the ones who gave him the state's electoral votes. The mayor of New York even refused to fly the American flag over City Hall on the day Lincoln was inaugurated. That all changed with his assassination, and the greatest day of mourning the city has ever seen took place when his coffin was laid in the very same City Hall in 1865.

The most beautiful statues honoring Civil War heroes were created and are now displayed in the city. Monuments by Augustus Saint-Gaudens, Daniel Chester French, Gutzon Borglum, and J. Q. A. Ward can be found here. The list is endless. *The Red Badge of Courage* was written here; *Dixie* was first sung here long before it became a Southern anthem; and John Wilkes Booth performed and lived here in the shadow of his famous actor brother, Edwin. There are also countless military relics here. Surprising to most people is the fact that many Civil War forts still dot the city, and in fact the star-shaped platform upon which the Statue of Liberty rests was once a Civil War fort. Mary Todd Lincoln went on her famous shopping sprees here; John Ericsson built the USS *Monitor* here; and General Grant wrote his memoirs here.

Q: Can you tell our readers a little about the photos? How you decided which photos to include, how long it took to gather them, etc.?

BM: Actually putting the photographs together was not a major problem. Since I visited each location several times during the course of the writing, I took many contemporary pictures of the sites. Historical sources were also used which documented the sites as they appeared 150 years ago. And of course, period books and magazines were a major resource. The only problems that arose during the production were taking pictures of current military bases, since this raises suspicion. But as soon as people learned that the pictures were for a Civil War book, they were most helpful.

Q: How or where did you conduct your research?

BM: I lived in New York City for more than 30 years and was active in historical research throughout the city. The New York Public Library was the prime source for information about the Civil War era and their collections, especially the map department, were essential. I also spent a good deal of time researching in the libraries of the New York Historical Society and the Museum of the City of New York. All these libraries offered support material for the actual job of visiting every possible location within the city limits. Those trips took me to every borough and quite a few of the harbor islands in the city.

Q: How long did it take you to conduct your research?

BM: The Civil War has been a lifelong interest, and for more than 25 years I have been collecting materials related to the Civil War sites in New York City.

Q: What is one thing about New York in the Civil War that you think will surprise readers?

BM: Most readers will be surprised to learn that New York City was largely pro-southern in her sympathies at the beginning of the war. As I mentioned before, the mayor of New York refused to fly the American flag over City Hall on the day of Lincoln's first inauguration. Many New Yorkers believed that war would be bad for their business, since many financial institutions were dependent upon the Southern investments in the city. I hope that readers will enjoy learning these lesser-known facts, and the wonderful Civil War history that New York City has to offer.

Q: Thank you for your time, we appreciate it.

BM: You're welcome.

Bibliography

Abbott, John S. C. *The History of the Civil War in America*. Springfield, MA: Gurdon Bill, 1863.

The American Anti-Slavery Almanac. New York: American Anti-Slavery Society, 1840.

Berman, Miriam. *Madison Square: The Park and Its Celebrated Landmarks*. Salt Lake City: Gibbs-Smith, 2001.

Booth, Mary L. *History of the City of New York*. New York: Clark & Meeker, 1859.

Brooks Brothers Centenary. New York: Brooks Brothers/Cheltenham Press, 1918.

Brooks, Elbridge Streeter. *The Story of New York*. Boston: D. Lothrop, 1888.

Brown, Henry Collins. *Book of Old New York*. New York: Privately printed, 1913.

Brown, Henry Collins, ed. *Valentine's Manual of Old New York, no. 5, new series, 1921*. New York: Valentine's Manual, 1920.

Bunyan, Patrick. *All Around the Town: Amazing Manhattan Facts and Curiosities*. New York: Fordham University Press, 1999.

Burnham, Alan, ed. *New York Landmarks*. Middletown, CT: Wesleyan University Press, 1963.

Burns, Ric, and James Sanders. *New York: An Illustrated History*. New York: Knopf, 1999.

Burrows, Edwin G., and Mike Wallace. Gotham: *A History of New York City to 1898*. New York: Oxford University Press, 1999.

Carroll, George D. *The Art of Dinner Giving, and Usages of Polite Society*. New York: Dempsey & Carroll, 1880.

Carroll, Raymond. *Barnes and Noble Complete Illustrated Map and Guidebook to Central Park*. New York: Barnes and Noble, 1999.

Clark, Emmons. *History of the Second Company of the Seventh Regiment (National Guard)*. New York: James G. Gregory, 1864.

Clarke, Asia Booth. *The Elder and Younger Booth*. Boston: Osgood, 1884.

Cook, Adrian. *The Armies of the Streets: The New York City Draft Riots of 1863*. Lexington, KY: University of Kentucky Press, 1974.

Cooke, Hope. *Seeking New York*. Philadelphia: Temple University Press, 1995.

Corbet, William. *New York Literary Lights*. Saint Paul, MN: Graywolf Press, 1998.

Cromie, Alice. *A Tour Guide to the Civil War*. Nashville, TN: Rutledge Hill Press, 1992.

Culbertson, Judi, and Tom Randall. *Permanent New Yorkers: A Biographical Guide to the Cemeteries of New York*. Chelsea, VT: Chelsea Green Publishing, 1987.

Dajani, Virginia. *Juror's Guide to Lower Manhattan: Six Walking Tours*. New York: Municipal Art Society, 1990.

Diamonstein, Barbaralee. *The Landmarks of New York III*. New York: Harry N. Abrams, 1998.

Dolkart, Andrew S., and Steven Wheeler. *Touring Lower Manhattan: Three Walks in New York's Historic Downtown*. New York: New York Landmarks Conservancy, 2000.

Edmiston, Susan, and Linda D Cirino. *Literary New York: A History and Guide*. Boston: Houghton Mifflin, 1976.

Ellis, Edward Robb. *The Epic of New York City: A Narrative History*. New York: Old Town Books, 1966.

Elson, Henry W. *The Civil War Through the Camera*. New York: McKinlay, Stone & Mackenzie, 1912.

Farley, John M. *History of St. Patrick's Cathedral*. New York: Society for the Propagation of the Faith, 1908.

Freudenheim, Ellen. Brooklyn: *Where to Go, What to Do, How to Get There*. New York: St. Martin's Press, 1991.

The Fugitive Slave Bill: Its History and Unconstitutionality. New York: William Harned, 1850.

Gayle, Margot, and Michele Cohen. *Guide to Manhattan's Outdoor Sculpture*. New York: Prentice Hall, 1988.

Gelbert, Doug. *Civil War Sites, Memorials, Museums and Library Collections*. Jefferson, NC: McFarland & Co., 1997.

Glickman, Toby and Gene. *The New York Red Pages: A Radical Tourist Guide*. New York: Praeger, 1984.

Godwin, Parke. *A Biography of William Cullen Bryant*. New York: Appleton, 1883.

Goldstone, Harmon H., and Martha Dalrymple. *History Preserved: A Guide to New York City Landmarks and Historic Districts*. New York: Simon and Schuster, 1974.

Goodale, Katherine. *Behind the Scenes with Edwin Booth*. Boston: Houghton Mifflin, 1931.

Greatorex, Eliza. *Old New York, from the Battery to Bloomingdale*. New York: Putnam, 1875.

Harper's Weekly (various dates)

Harris, M. A. *A Negro History Tour of Manhattan*. New York: Greenwood, 1968.

Headley, J. T. *The Great Rebellion*. Hartford: Hurlbut, Williams & Co., 1863.

Heckscher, Morrison H. "Creating Central Park." Metropolitan Museum of Art Bulletin, vol. 65, no. 3 (Winter 2008).

Henneke, Ben Graf. *Laura Keene: A Biography*. Tulsa, OK: Council Oak Books, 1990.

Holzer, Harold, ed. *Lincoln and New York*. New York: New York Historical Society, 2009.

Horan, James D. *Mathew Brady: Historian with a Camera*. New York: Bonanza Books, 1955.

Illustrated London News (various dates).

Israelowitz, Oscar. *Lower East Side Tourbook*. 6th ed. Brooklyn: Israelowitz Publishing, 1998.

Jackson, Kenneth T., ed. *The Encyclopedia of New York City*. New Haven: Yale University Press, 1995.

Johnson, Clint. "A Vast and Fiendish Plot": The Confederate Attack on New York City. New York: Citadel Press, 2010.

Kayton, Bruce. *Radical Walking Tours of New York City*. New York: Seven Stories Press, 1999.

Keegan, John. *The American Civil War: A Military History*. New York: Vintage, 2009.

Kelley, Frank Bergen. *Historical Guide to the City of New York*. New York: Frederic A. Stokes Co., 1909.

Keneally, Thomas. *American Scoundrel*. London: Chatto & Windus, 2002.

Lederer, Joseph. *All Around the Town: A Walking Guide to Outdoor Sculpture in New York City*. New York: Scribner's, 1975.

Limmer, Ruth. *Six Heritage Tours of the Lower East Side*. New York: New York University Press, 1997.

Lossing, Benson J. *A History of the Civil War and the Causes That Led Up to the Great Conflict*. New York: War Memorial Association, 1912.

McCabe, James D. *New York by Gaslight*. New York: Greenwich House, reprint of 1882 edition.

McKay, Ernest A. *The Civil War and New York City*. Syracuse, NY: Syracuse University Press, 1990.

Mendelsohn, Joyce. *Touring the Flatiron: Walks in Four Historic Neighborhoods*. New York: New York Landmarks Conservancy, 1998.

Miller, Terry. *Greenwich Village and How It Got That Way*. New York: Crown, 1990.

Miller's New York As It Is; or Stranger's Guide-Book to the Cities of New York, Brooklyn and Adjacent Places. New York: James Miller, 1863.

Moore, Margaret. *End of the Road for Ladies' Mile?* New York: Municipal Art Society of New York, 1986.

Morris, Roy, Jr. *The Better Angel: Walt Whitman in the Civil War*. New York: Oxford University Press, 2000.

Moscow, Henry. *The Street Book: An Encyclopedia of Manhattan's Street Names and Their Origins*. New York: Hagstrom, 1978.

New York Monuments Commission. *New York at Gettysburg*. Albany: J. B. Lyon, 1900.

New York Times (various dates)

Nicolay, John G., and John Hay. *Abraham Lincoln: A History*. New York: Century Co., 1890.

Northrop, Henry Davenport. *Life and Deeds of General Sherman*. Boston: B. B. Russell, 1891.

The Obsequies of Abraham Lincoln in the City of New York. New York: Edmund Jones, 1866.

Plotch, Batia, ed. *New York Walks.* New York: Henry Holt, 1992.

Prince, Cathryn J. *Burn the Town and Sack the Banks!* New York: Carroll & Graf, 2006.

Reynolds, Donald Martin. *Monuments and Masterpieces: Histories and Views of Public Sculpture in New York City.* New York: Macmillan Publishing Co., 1988.

Sears, Stephen W. *George B. McClellan: The Young Napoleon.* New York: Ticknor and Fields, 1988.

Seeman, Helene Zucker, and Alanna Siegfried. *Soho.* New York: Neal-Schuman, 1978.

Seitz, Sharon, and Stuart Miller. *The Other Islands of New York City.* Woodstock, VT: The Countryman Press, 1995.

Seyfried, Vincent F., and William Asadorian. *Old Queens, New York in Early Photographs.* Mineola, NY: Dover, 1991.

Shaw, Albert. *Abraham Lincoln: His Path to the Presidency.* New York: Review of Reviews, 1929.

——. *Abraham Lincoln: The Year of His Election.* New York: Review of Reviews, 1930.

Shepard, Richard F. *Broadway from the Battery to the Bronx.* New York: Harry N. Abrams, 1987.

Soodalter, Ron. *Hanging Captain Gordon: The Life and Trial of an American Slave Trader.* New York: Atria Books, 2006.

Spann, Edward K. *Gotham at War: New York City, 1860-1865.* Wilmington, DE: Scholarly Resources, 2002.

Still, Bayrd. *Mirror for Gotham: New York as seen by contemporaries from Dutch days to the present.* New York: Washington Square University Press, 1956.

Stowe, Harriet Beecher. *Men of Our Times; or Leading Patriots of the Day.* New York: J. D. Denison, 1868.

Swanberg, W. A. *Sickles the Incredible.* New York: Charles Scribner's Sons, 1956.

Titone, Nora. *My Thoughts Be Bloody.* New York: Free Press, 2010.

Ulmann, Albert. *A Landmark History of New York.* New York: Appleton Century, 1939.

Union League Club of New York. New York: Union League Club, 1918.

Valentine, D. T. *Manual of the Corporation of the City of New York: 1863.* New York: Clerk's Office, 1863.

——. *Manual of the Corporation of the City of New York: 1864.* New York: Clerk's Office, 1864.

——. *Manual of the Corporation of the City of New York: 1865.* New York: Clerk's Office, 1865.

Voorsanger, Catherine Hoover, and John K. Howat. *Art and the Empire City: New York, 1825-1861.* New York: Metropolitan Museum, 2000.

Wetherby, John. *Lloyd's Pocket companion and guide through New York City, for 1866-67.* New York: Thomas Lloyd, 1866.

White, Norval, and Elliot Willensky. *AIA Guide to New York City.* 4th ed. New York: Three Rivers Press, 2000.

Wilson, H. *Trow's New York City Directory, vol. 71.* New York: John F. Trow, 1856.

Wilson, Richard Guy. *McKim, Mead & White Architects.* New York: Rizzoli, 1983.

Wilson, Rufus Rockwell. *New York in Literature: The story told in the landmarks of town and country.* Elmira, NY: Primavera Press, 1947.

Wolfe, Gerard R. New York: *A Guide to the Metropolis, Walking Tours of Architecture and History.* New York: McGraw-Hill, 1988.

Index

About the Author

Photo credit: Chris Felver

Bill Morgan is a writer, editor, and archival consultant who has lived in New York City for more than thirty years. He is the author of more than two dozen guidebooks and texts including *Literary Landmarks of New York*. His most recent book, *The Typewriter Is Holy*, was published by Simon & Schuster in 2010. Since the 1970s he has worked as an archivist and librarian.